ROLL CALL

SPIRITUAL INSIGHTS BENEATH THE BLUE LIGHTS

HAROLD SAVAGE

WestBow
PRESS
DIVISION OF THOMAS NELSON

WestBow Press books may be ordered through booksellers or by contacting:

WestBow Press
A Division of Thomas Nelson
1663 Liberty Drive
Bloomington, IN 47403
www.westbowpress.com
1-(866) 928-1240

ISBN: 978-1-4497-7843-9 (sc)
ISBN: 978-1-4497-7844-6 (hc)
ISBN: 978-1-4497-7842-2 (e)

Library of Congress Control Number: 2012923216

Printed in the United States of America

WestBow Press rev. date: 12/11/2012

To my wife, Kay, whom I dearly love and who, from the example of her life, has taught me to teach the truth in love, enjoy the journey, and that with God, all things are possible. Thank you for saying yes more than thirty years ago!

To my son and daughter, Larry and Michelle—you have made being a father a joy and a privilege. I love you with all of my heart. By honoring God with your lives, you have honored your mother and me.

To my mother, June, who taught me to read, write, and love the Bible. Thank you, Mom, for always seeing the potential and never giving up. I love you.

To the law enforcement community—I was privileged to be a part of your family for only a few years, but the profound impact of that experience has lasted a lifetime. Thank you for serving and protecting.

Contents

A special thanks to Lynette Carnahan Gray, author of *Letters of Hope,* for encouraging me to write and reading and analyzing the original manuscript.

Thank you, Monty Joseph, Carl Head, and Kay Savage, for reading and rereading the *Roll Call* manuscript. Your constant encouragement made me work harder at the self-discipline of writing.

I want to thank the elders and congregation that calls me its preacher. You have helped shape my life, and I love you. It has been a pleasure to be coworkers in God's vineyard for over twenty years.

Finally, I would like to thank God, who made me, saved me, and blesses me every day. To Him I give all the glory!

ROLL CALL

Spiritual Insights Beneath the Blue Lights

Reporting for Duty

The police roll call, or as it's sometimes referred to, the lineup, is a brief meeting at the beginning of every police officer's shift or watch. The purpose is threefold: one, to simply check the number present; two, to inspect whether officers are appropriately and professionally dressed; and three, to prepare officers with information and guidance they will need to carry out their duties safely and successfully.

This book is your spiritual roll call. You have reported for duty, and you must be alert. For this spiritual lineup, you must be professionally equipped, having "put on the full armor of God," (Ephesians 6:11 NIV) and now you must be briefed so you can be prepared to carry out your duty with the success and safety that only heaven can provide.

In most police departments, a supervisor, generally a Sergeant, is in charge of the briefing. In this roll call, God will conduct the briefing through His Word. Imagine—the highest-ranking supervisor in the universe will provide you with vital information. The maker and sustainer of all things will give you what you need to not just survive, but also thrive during your tour of duty.

It doesn't matter if you are on the day shift, evenings, or the night watch. God will be there with you, and His words will instruct you.

"He who keeps you will not slumber. Behold, He who keeps Israel will neither slumber nor sleep" (Psalm 121:3b–4 NASB).

You Have the Right to Remain Silent
The Power of Our Words

As a minister, I have learned the incredible power of well-timed words. Working as a police officer before cell phones, computers in police cars, and long before Tasers, I learned the importance of the manner one employs to speak those words. With your words, you can bring calm to a situation or create chaos. With your words, you can cause a person to surrender without a fight or pick a fight. With your words, you can defuse situations that are potentially harmful or incite a riot.

When the police interrogate suspects, they must advise them of their rights prior to any questioning. It's called "The Miranda." The following is a minimal Miranda warning, as outlined in the Supreme Court's 1966 ruling, *Miranda v. Arizona*.

You have the right to remain silent. Anything you say can and will be used against you in a court of law. You have the right to speak to an attorney, and to have an attorney present during any questioning. If you cannot afford a lawyer, one will be provided for you at government expense.

Listen to the power of this phrase: "Anything you say can and will be used against you ..." Many people have never realized the tremendous power and influence of their words.

As a minister, I found my livelihood dependent upon my words. I have learned that there is great power in the words I speak and the words I write. I am accountable for my words. I must be careful as I choose those words. *How* I say something is just as important as *what* I say.

Police officers carry lethal and non-lethal weapons. They know that long before they draw their guns, they do their level best to talk reasonably with people. As my dad used to say, "You try to talk some sense into them." A police officer must know the weapons at his or her disposal, because each situation demands a different degree of force.

I arrested the same man twice in the same year—both times for burglary. The first time, he had broken into a construction business, tripping the silent alarm. The last time I arrested him, he was breaking into cars in the parking garage of a downtown hotel. He was easy to remember, because he was *big!* He was so big that I could barely get the handcuffs around his wrists. The first time I arrested him, I had the help of half a dozen policemen, but the second time, I was alone with him in that parking garage.

I remember praying, "Lord, I may have to shoot this guy if he resists, so please, Lord, help me say the right things." Thank God the suspect gave up without a fight.

The Bible says, "A gentle answer turns away wrath, but a harsh word stirs up anger" and "A man has joy in an apt answer, and how delightful is a timely word!" (Proverbs 15:1, 23 NASB).

Domestic disputes present some of the worst situations to law enforcement officials. Each situation is different, but every one of them is dangerous. You may try to resolve a conflict between a wife and husband, a boyfriend and girlfriend, or a dad and daughter. The closeness of the relationship makes the situation even more volatile. Small children are often present, listening, and affected by the outcome. Long before the police arrive at those homes, words are spoken. These individuals could have stopped the verbal abuse. Long before the police arrived, they could have spoken words of kindness and apology instead of threats and words of hate and anger. But they chose not to.

Earlier I referred to our words as "non-lethal" weapons, but that really isn't true. The old adage, "sticks and stones may break my bones but words will never hurt me," just isn't accurate. The Bible says that "Death and life are in the power of the tongue" (Proverbs 18:21 NASB). James wrote that the "tongue also is a fire, a world of evil among the parts of the body. It corrupts the whole person, sets the whole course of his life on fire, and is itself set on fire by hell" (James 3:6 NIV). That does not sound like the use of "non-lethal" words, does it?

In the book of Proverbs, Solomon painted an incredible picture for us: "Reckless words pierce like a sword, but the tongue of the wise brings healing" (Proverbs 12:18 NIV). Using reckless words is like attacking someone with a knife and stabbing that person over and over. But the timely use of wise words is like an ointment that brings healing.

You don't have to be a salesman, preacher, politician, or policeman to practice the power of well-timed words. In every relationship at home, work, or church, you must learn the power of your words. Choose the words you speak wisely, because according to Jesus, we will give an account for every careless word.

> The good man brings good things out of the good stored up in him, and the evil man brings evil things out of the evil stored up in him. But I tell you that men will have to give account on the day of judgment for every careless word they have spoken. For by your words you will be acquitted, and by your words you will be condemned. (Matthew 12:35–37 NIV)

Jesus brings a whole new meaning to the Miranda phrase, "Anything you say can and will be used against you in a court of law." One day, the highest of all courts will take into account the words that each of us has spoken.

I love what the apostle Paul wrote to the Ephesians when he said, "not to let any unwholesome word proceed from your mouth but only such a word as is good for edification according to the need of the moment, that it may give grace to those that hear" (Ephesians 4:29 NASB).

According to Paul, our words actually have the power to build people up and extend grace. When you encourage with your words, you instill courage in others. When you discourage with your words, you remove courage from them. Proverbs 15:4 counsels, "The tongue that brings healing is a tree of life, but a deceitful tongue crushes the spirit" (NASB). Our families and the people around us desperately need to hear encouraging, faith-building, life-giving words. Please speak them!

The Miranda statement begins, "You have the right to remain silent." This is prudent advice for all of us! How many times have we regretted our words? As soon as they tumbled past our lips, we could do nothing to retrieve them. If only we had kept quiet. Solomon wrote, "A man of knowledge uses words with restraint, and a man of understanding is even-tempered. Even a fool is thought wise if he keeps silent, and discerning if he holds his tongue" (Proverbs 17:27–28 NIV).

James wrote, "Take note of this: Everyone should be quick to listen, slow to speak and slow to become angry" (James 1:19 NIV). Part of growing up, maturing, and practicing self-control is the ability to be in command of our words. Again, the book of Proverbs teaches us, "A fool always loses his temper, but a wise man holds it back" (Proverbs 29:11 NASB).

In the Old Testament, 1 Samuel 25 relates an interesting story about Nabal, Abigail, and David, the soon-to-be king. The Bible tells us that Nabal was a wealthy, foolish man and that his wife, Abigail, was intelligent and beautiful. David and his men provided a type of police security for the shepherds of Nabal and other wealthy landowners in the region. In return, those landowners fed David and his men. In a very kind and courteous manner, David's men traveled to Nabal's home so that they might collect some supplies from Nabal. True to his foolish character, Nabal insulted them and sent them on their way empty-handed. When David heard about what Nabal had said and done, he strapped on his sword and led an army of four hundred men storming toward Nabal's house to destroy him and all of his male servants.

In the meantime, Abigail got wind of how Nabal had treated David's men. Immediately, she gathered together a large load of provisions, loaded them onto some donkeys, and took them to David and his men.

You can read this account for yourself in 1 Samuel 25:20–35. As Abigail descended into a mountain ravine, David and his men confronted her. Abigail dismounted and bowed to the ground. She apologized to David and reminded him that when he became King of Israel, he certainly would not want this act of vengeance on his resume.

David then said to Abigail,

"Praise be to the LORD, the God of Israel, who has sent you today to meet me. May you be blessed for your good judgment and for keeping me from bloodshed this day and from avenging myself with my own hands. Otherwise, as surely as the LORD, the God of Israel, lives, who has kept me from harming you, if you had not come quickly to meet me, not one male belonging to Nabal would have been left alive by daybreak." Then David accepted from her hand what she had brought him and said, "Go home in peace. I have heard your words and granted your request." (1 Samuel 25:32–35 NIV)

Talk about the awesome power of our words! A solitary woman traveled with some donkeys packed with provisions. By speaking a handful of words, she managed to disarm a great warrior like David and turn back his army of four hundred. With her words, she saved the lives of her family and friends and salvaged the reputation of the future king of Israel. Nabal's foolish words incited the wrath of an army, while Abigail's discerning words negotiated a peaceful resolution and saved lives.

I want to suggest several things that could help you with your words:

1. Words begin in the heart, so if you want to get serious about changing your life-taking words into life-giving words, then change your heart. You are only treating the symptom if you do anything less. Jesus said, "But the things that come out of the mouth come from the heart, and these make a man unclean" (Matthew 15:18 NIV).

2. Set a guard on your mouth, and filter your words. The psalmist prayed, "Set a guard over my mouth, O LORD; keep watch over the door of my lips" (Psalm 141:3 NASB). The Bible pictures us placing a sentry or guard at the door of our words. Before you say anything or write anything on Facebook, Twitter, or e-mail, try sifting or filtering those words through Ephesians 4:29, and ask, *Is what I am about to say or write going to build up or tear down? Will this bring grace to those who hear or read it?*

As hard as this may seem, when in doubt, don't say anything! Your mother gave you good advice when she told you, "If you can't say something nice, don't say anything at all."

3. Memorize the last verse in Psalm 19, and allow that verse to be your prayer every morning. Before you begin your day, pray, "Let the words of my mouth and the meditation of my heart be acceptable in Thy sight, O LORD, my Rock and my Redeemer" (Psalm 19:14 NASB).

Words are my livelihood. Truth be told, since "death and life are in the power of the tongue," words are your livelihood, too. When you decide to speak, let your words be wholesome, uplifting, and gracious. When you don't think your words will achieve that objective, remember that you have the right to remain silent.

Questions for discussion and a call to action:

1. What do you believe are the most discouraging words a person could hear? What do you believe are the most encouraging words a person could hear?

2. Has there ever been a time in your life when you were discouraged and someone spoke encouraging words to you? What was the circumstance, and what was said?

3. Which do you think is likely to cause the greater hurt in a person's life—sticks and stones or words? Why?

4. Read James 3:1–12. Note there how the tongue has the ability to direct, destroy, and delight. James pointed out (v. 9) that both blessing and cursing can come out of the very same mouth. What effects could these *conflicting* words have on the ones hearing them? On the one saying them? On God, who hears all of what is said?

5. For the next thirty days, determine to think before you speak. Do not gossip. Do not respond with sarcasm. Choose your words carefully before you express them. Look for ways to encourage.

6. Memorize Psalm 19:14: "May the words of my mouth and the meditation of my heart be pleasing in your sight, O LORD, my Rock and my Redeemer."

Spiritual Weapons and Tactics
The Power of Knowing Our Enemy

Special Weapons and Tactics (SWAT) teams are small, specially trained and equipped groups of law enforcement officials deployed during explosive or high-risk situations. Such situations can involve dealing with barricaded suspects or serving warrants on particularly violent offenders. SWAT teams are usually composed of the elite members of a police department or other law enforcement agency. To help them in their job, SWAT teams use a large and varied arsenal of weapons. (Quote from an article entitled, *Weapons Used by SWAT Teams* written by: Michael Wolfe)

D id you know that every day, you and I are engaged in a spiritual warfare? We have an enemy, and he wants to destroy us or at least render us useless in our desire to obey God's will for our lives.

Robert Greene's book *The 33 Strategies of War* opens with a powerful statement: "Life is an endless battle and conflict, and you cannot fight effectively unless you can identify your enemies." I love the famous quote from Sun Tzu in *The Art of War:* "If you know the enemy and know yourself, you need not fear the result of a hundred battles. If you know yourself but not the enemy, for every victory gained you will also suffer a defeat. If you know neither the enemy nor yourself, you will succumb in every battle."

While these quotes were made in reference to physical, military battles, the spiritual application is even more significant. You and I need to know about our spiritual enemy. First Peter 5:8 tells us to "Be alert and of sober mind. Your enemy the devil prowls around like a roaring lion looking for someone to devour" (NIV). Not long ago in Zanesville, Ohio, the owner of an exotic animal farm took his own life after turning loose dozens of lions, tigers, and other beasts. Sheriff's deputies with high-powered rifles were forced to kill many of these animals that had been set free. When interviewed, the local sheriff likened a lion in the wild to a loaded gun. When the Bible describes our enemy as a "lion seeking to devour," it is warning us of a dangerous and formidable adversary.

Jesus explained in John 8:44 that the Devil "was a murderer from the beginning, and does not stand in the truth because there is no truth in him. Whenever he speaks a lie, he speaks from his own nature, for he is a liar and the father of lies" (NIV). No wonder Paul encouraged us in Ephesians 6:10–11 to "be strong in the Lord and in His mighty power. Put on the full armor of God, so that you can take your stand against the devil's schemes."

There is an unseen reality. There is an unseen battle being waged all around us. The apostle Paul wrote, "For our struggle is not against flesh and blood, but against the rulers, against the authorities, against the powers of this dark world and against the spiritual forces of evil in the heavenly realms" (Ephesians 6:12 NIV).

This battle cannot be fought with conventional weapons: "For though we live in the world, we do not wage war as the world does. The weapons we fight with are not the weapons of the world. On the contrary, they have divine power to demolish strongholds" (2 Corinthians 10:3–4 NIV).

There is no real safety or security apart from our Lord. The psalmist prayed, "Keep me safe, O God, for in you I take refuge. I said to the LORD, "You are my Lord; apart from you I have no good thing" (Psalm 16:1–2 NIV).

In the Old Testament, you can read the story about the king of Aram being at war with Israel. Every time the king of Aram made an offensive move, Israel would counter it or thwart it in some way. Israel somehow knew in advance of Aram's troop movements, when they were going to strike and where they had set an ambush. It happened so often that the king of Aram was convinced that Aram had a mole. But the king's men assured him that there was no spy but instead a prophet in Israel named Elisha: a "prophet who … tells the king of Israel the very words you speak in your bedroom" (2 Kings 6:12 NIV).

When the king of Aram heard about this prophet, he ordered his army to track down Elisha and capture him! They found Elisha in Dothan, and under the cover of night, the king's massive army surrounded the city. In 2 Kings 6:15–17, we read what transpired.

When the servant of the man of God got up and went out early the next morning, an army with horses and chariots had surrounded the city. "Oh, my lord, what shall we do?" the servant asked. "Don't be afraid," the prophet answered. "Those who are with us are more than those who are with them." And Elisha prayed, "O LORD, open his eyes so he may see." Then the LORD opened the servant's eyes, and he looked and saw the hills full of horses and chariots of fire all around Elisha" (NIV).

This story reminds us that there is an unseen reality. God's people are never alone, and according to 2 Kings 6, they are never outnumbered. Much like the servant of Elisha, we are oblivious to the unseen world all around us. So let each of us pray, "Open our eyes, Lord, that we may see that we are in a real, spiritual battle. Open our eyes to see our unseen resources. Open our eyes to see our ever-present help on the horizon."

The unseen battle, won or lost, has eternal consequences: "So we fix our eyes not on what is seen, but on what is unseen. For what is seen is temporary, but what is unseen is eternal" (2 Corinthians 4:18 NIV).

Did you know that the reigning champion and undefeated King of kings fights on our behalf? Before his battle with Goliath, David told Saul, "The Lord who delivered me from the paw of the lion and the paw of the bear will deliver me from the hand of this Philistine" (1 Samuel 17:37 NIV). David said to the giant warrior Goliath in the Valley of Elah, "All those gathered here will know that it is not by sword or spear that the Lord saves; for the battle is the Lord's, and he will give all of you into our hands" (1 Samuel 17:47 NIV).

No wonder we are repeatedly admonished in God's Word to "walk by faith, not by sight" (2 Corinthians 5:7 NASB). If you can see it then it's not faith, because "faith is the assurance of things hoped for, the conviction of things not seen" (Hebrews

11:1 NASB). According to the writer of Hebrews, Moses must have seen the unseen, because it was by "faith he left Egypt, not fearing the king's anger; he persevered because He saw Him who is invisible" (Hebrews 11:27 NIV).

Just because the conflict cannot be seen doesn't make the threat any less factual. So arm yourself with the weapons that can actually make a difference in your daily spiritual conflicts. In Ephesians 6, we are told to put on God's armor, and we find a checklist of spiritual weapons. When you read Ephesians 6:14–20, you will notice the continual sources of spiritual power. Working in union with each other, we find the Holy Spirit, prayer, and the Word of God. God's Spirit will give us the strength needed for our daily battles, and no Christian can experience victory without these weapons.

In military battles as well as our spiritual battles, there is a time to retreat and a time to stand and fight. The Bible tells us to "[f]lee from sexual immorality. All other sins a person commits are outside the body, but whoever sins sexually, sins against their own body" (1 Corinthians 6:18 NIV). In 1 Corinthians 10:14, Paul told the church to "flee from idolatry." And in 2 Timothy, he wrote, "Flee the evil desires of youth and pursue righteousness, faith, love and peace, along with those who call on the Lord out of a pure heart" (2 Timothy 2:22–23 NIV).

There is a time in our spiritual battles when the most reasonable action to take is to retreat. That's what Joseph did. According to Genesis 39, Joseph was pursued by the wife of his master, Potiphar. Joseph managed to dodge her advances for a time, and then one day, she cornered him in the house and grabbed hold of his garments. Joseph did the right thing; he retreated. That may be an understatement. Joseph ran like Usain Bolt runs for the finish line!

First Corinthians 10:13 gives us a great promise in fighting this spiritual battle: "No temptation has overtaken you but such as is common to man; and God is faithful, who will not allow you to be tempted beyond what you are able, but with the temptation will provide the way of escape also, so that you will be able to endure it" (NASB). We need to look for that way of escape.

While retreating is wise and many times the best course of action, there are times when we must take a stand and fight the good fight. There are some things still worth fighting for. Fight for your faith. Fight for your integrity. Fight for truth. The apostle Paul summed up his life with these words: "I have fought the good fight, I have finished the course, I have kept the faith" (2 Timothy 4:7 NASB). Vern Jocque said, "You might as well stand and fight because if you run, you will only die tired."

When I think of standing and fighting, I think of an Old Testament warrior named Shammah. Shammah was one of King David's greatest soldiers, known as the "mighty men." The biblical record introduces Shammah to us with a brief but amazing story.

> Next to him was Shammah, son of Agee the Hararite. When the Philistines banded together at a place where there was a field full of lentils, Israel's troops fled from them. But Shammah took his stand in the middle of the field. He defended it and struck the Philistines down, and the Lord brought about a great victory. (2 Samuel 23:11–12 NIV)

Why did Shammah take a stand against the Philistines and defend a bean patch when everyone else deserted him on the field of battle? I believe that Shammah defended what mattered to him most. I am not sure what strategic value that plot of land held for Shammah, but it was worth the fight, so he took a stand. Remember in war, whatever you surrender will become more difficult if not impossible to recover. If the Philistines captured Shammah's small piece of land, then they could take any adjacent property along with it. So he fought for a field of beans in order to keep the enemy from further encroachment.

This is what our spiritual enemy does. He encroaches in small, subtle areas in our lives and captures whatever territory we surrender to him. He is always looking to advance and never tires of the battle. Paul said in Ephesians 4:27, "Don't give the devil an opportunity." The Devil is always looking for an opportunity to take whatever ground you may surrender.

Spiritual soldiers use spiritual weapons. Fighting a spiritual battle without being a spiritual soldier is like a civilian fighting crime while impersonating a police officer. He has no authority and therefore no power to carry out his duty. God's great claim according to His Word is that "'No weapon that is formed against you will prosper; and every tongue that accuses you in judgment you will condemn. This is the heritage of the servants of the LORD, and their vindication is from Me,' declares the LORD" (Isaiah 54:17 NASB).

If you have knowledge that there is an enemy, and you know he is going to attack you, then it stands to reason that you will prepare yourself for that spiritual conflict, and you will be ready to defend yourself to fight the good fight of faith. The Bible teaches us to "Resist the Devil, and he will flee from you" (James 4:7 NASB). Isaiah said that "When the enemy comes in like a flood, the Spirit of the Lord will lift up a standard against him" (Isaiah 59:19 NKJV).

Have you heard the expression "to be forewarned is to be forearmed"? I want to forewarn you of where our enemy will attack us. Let me suggest to you that the battlefield is your mind and that these spiritual battles will be won and lost contingent upon our thinking. The enemy attacks us within our minds—our thought lives. Paul wrote in Romans 8:5, "Those who live according to the flesh have their minds set on what the flesh desires; but those who live in accordance with the Spirit have their minds set on what the Spirit desires" (NIV).

You and I are responsible for our thought lives. You and I are the only ones who have control over our thought processes. Solomon said it best in Proverbs 23:7: "For as he thinks within himself, so he is." Who we are today is due in large part to our thinking yesterday. We become what we think about. We move toward our dominant thoughts. We are the sum total of our past and present thoughts. If you want to change the way you act, then change the way you think. Our actions are the direct result of our thinking. That is a great description of repentance: a change of mind that leads to a change of heart, which leads to a change in direction.

God tells us that we can change our thinking. You and I can renovate our minds. "Present your bodies a living sacrifice, holy, acceptable to God, which is your reasonable service. And do not be conformed to this world, but be transformed by the renewing of your mind, that you may prove what is that good and acceptable and perfect will of God" (Romans 12:1–2 NJKV).

Please allow me to make some suggestions to help in fighting this spiritual battle. First of all, acknowledge that there is a spiritual conflict. Acknowledge that there is a real adversary who wants to destroy you, your marriage, your health, and your home. This helps to put our daily conflicts into their proper perspective. Our battle is not against flesh and blood. Our battle is not with our spouse, neighbor, or boss. Much of our daily personal conflict is nothing more than symptoms of the spiritual conflict that comes from having a spiritual enemy.

Second, know how the enemy operates. Be aware of his schemes. It is not a sin to be tempted, but it becomes sin as we surrender to that temptation. James tells us that "each person is tempted when they are dragged away by their own evil desire and enticed. Then, after desire has conceived, it gives birth to sin; and sin, when it is full-grown, gives birth to death" (James 1:14–15 NIV). James painted for us a picture of Satan as a fisherman who always casts bait into our paths.

Third, you must guard and protect the gate by which the enemy always arrives. Remember, the gate is the mind. The enemy enters through the doorway of our thinking. No wonder Paul told the church at Philippi, "Finally, brothers and sisters, whatever is true, whatever is noble, whatever is right, whatever is pure, whatever is lovely, whatever is admirable—if anything is excellent or praiseworthy—think about such things" (Philippians 4:8 NIV). Paul also said that we must not be conformed to this world, but we are to be transformed through our *minds* (Romans 12:2). If you are serious about changing the way you are living, then change the way you think! I love this promise from Isaiah: "Thou wilt keep him in perfect peace, whose mind is stayed on Thee, because he trusts in Thee" (Isaiah 26:3 KJV).

Finally, remember that Satan is a defeated foe. Hebrews 2:14–15 tells us, "Since the children have flesh and blood, he too shared in their humanity so that by his death he might break the power of him who holds the power of death—that is, the devil—and free those who all their lives were held in slavery by their fear of death" (NIV). The only power that the Devil has over our lives is the power that we allow him to have. In other words, we are not helpless Christians who are always surrendering in the heat of this ongoing conflict. Satan can only take what we give to him.

First John 4:4 tells us, "You, dear children, are from God and have overcome them, because the One who is in you is greater than the one who is in the world." Again, I want to remind you of David's words to Goliath: "It is not by sword or spear that the Lord saves; for the battle is the Lord's."

Questions for discussion and a call to action:

1. Name some of the subtle, deceptive ways that Satan lies to us.

2. In what ways should our battle strategy change as we acknowledge that our battle is with Satan and not with each other?

3. Like the warrior, Shammah, in 2 Samuel 23, what field in your life do you believe is still worth defending? Specifically, how are you going to defend it?

4. How can you put into practice Paul's challenge to the church at Philippi, as he told them to let their minds dwell on the right kinds of things? "Whatever is true, whatever is noble, whatever is right, whatever is pure, whatever is lovely, whatever is admirable—if anything is excellent or praiseworthy—think about such things" (Philippians 4:8 NIV).

5. Because the spiritual battle that we are involved in cannot be fought with conventional weapons, will you make it a habit to pray and read a portion of God's Word (the Spirit's sword) every day?

6. Memorize 1 Corinthians 10:13: "No temptation has overtaken you but such as is common to man; and God is faithful, who will not allow you to be tempted beyond what you are able, but with the temptation will provide the way of escape also, so that you will be able to endure it" (NASB).

3

There Is a Little "Fife" in All of Us
The Power of Learning from Our Mistakes

As a young police officer, I made many mistakes. While no police officer tries to model himself after Barney Fife, I'm sure that like me, many police officers, on occasion, have felt like Barney. Even if you have never been a police officer, you may identify with Barney, because I think that there is a little "Fife" in all of us.

You remember Barney Fife, don't you? He was a character played by the great comedian Don Knotts in the 1960s sitcom *The Andy Griffith Show.* Barney Fife served as the Deputy Sheriff for the town of Mayberry, and he made many mistakes. Unlike Barney, I was issued more than one bullet, but very much like the loveable character Don Knotts won five Emmy Awards portraying, I made some pretty silly mistakes. I love the character Barney Fife, because I think I can identify with him. He had a great heart and always had good intentions, but occasionally he would stick his foot in his mouth and really mess things up.

It does not matter what you endeavor to do with your life; mistakes will be made. Many people never pursue their dreams or attempt anything outside their comfort zones because of a fear of failure or a fear that they may be embarrassed. Remember that the goal is to give your best and do your best. We certainly should set the bar high and strive for perfection but never fall apart because of failure.

When I speak of mistakes, I'm not talking about deliberate, sinful action. According to Bing Dictionary the word *mistake* is defined as "an incorrect, unwise, or unfortunate act or decision caused by bad judgment or a lack of information or care." In the natural process of living our lives, we will make mistakes and find ourselves in embarrassing situations. In football, if you run with the ball enough, you are going to fumble. In basketball, if you shoot the ball enough, you are going to eventually shoot an air ball. Successful athletes don't let the fear of those things keep them from running and shooting.

I had watched enough police movies and television cop shows by the time I became a police officer to know that the really good cops were able to chase down the bad guys and solve every crime with *perfection.* The problem with real-life situations is that we rarely do anything to perfection. Even the reality shows on television today are edited.

As a police officer, I made many mistakes and experienced many embarrassing moments. I will just choose a few to share with you, and after you are finished laughing with me and not at me, I will tell you what I have learned from those experiences.

As a rookie patrolman, the first year is a year of probation for being trained and evaluated. Of course, you want to perform well before your supervisors. Chief Barnes was a real stickler for the police hat being part of the police uniform. When I exited my police cruiser, I had to have my hat on. I hated wearing a hat. You can imagine how I felt while writing an accident report at a downtown bus station when the Chief of Police brought me my hat. He had retrieved it from my police car. Chief William Barnes was a great chief and a very fair man, but I had never been chewed out professionally until he did it. That being said, one of my most embarrassing moments came several months later while working the midnight shift.

I was the first officer to arrive on the scene of a reported intoxicated man walking down the middle of the street with a knife. As I pulled onto the road where the man was supposed to be, he walked right out onto the roadway directly into my path, knife in hand, swearing about something that made very little sense. As I exited my cruiser, I remembered the behind-chewing that I had received from the Chief, which made me remember my hat. I reached back against the Plexiglas shield where my hat rested, retrieved it, and put it on my head. In my most intimidating voice, I ordered the man to drop the knife, and he immediately complied.

A crowd started to gather on both sides of the street, and I gave them orders to stay back. By then, two other police officers who were sent to cover me arrived. I noticed they were looking at me oddly as I went to apprehend the intoxicated man. When I moved to put my handcuffs on him, he moved away and said something about my not knowing what I was doing because of my hat. Before I figured it out on my own, the man reached up, grabbed my hat off my head, and looked at me through the rim of my hat. Apparently as I pulled my hat from its resting place inside the police car, I had inadvertently pulled the entire top of the hat completely off and was just wearing the rim of the hat! The covering police officers were laughing so hard that they couldn't even help me handcuff my knife-wielding friend.

Policemen never forget anything. You *never* live anything down, and that mistakes and embarrassing moments are talked about *forever!*

I have lived through many awkward moments, like the time I was called to a downtown hotel to help a confused elderly man who had walked into the hotel lobby after straying from a care home nearby. I just thought it would be a routine act of kindness; I would drive the man back to his nursing home. Not with this old-timer! As I attempted to escort him out of the hotel lobby and into the back of my police car, the man began acting crazy and started beating me with his cane. I wasn't about to call for backup, because he was ninety years old! That man beat me all over that lobby.

My own mother was on her way to the Palm Beach Mall, stopped in the middle of one of the busiest intersections in our city, where I was directing traffic around a three-car traffic accident. She told me to "get out of the road before I injured myself." After I threatened to arrest her, she got mad and drove off in a huff.

Let's face it; if you endeavor anything with your life, you will make mistakes and experience moments that you would just as soon forget. Over the years, I have encountered many people who are afraid to step out in faith and tackle their dreams simply because they are afraid they will mess up in front of someone else. Trust me—you will mess up! That is just part of accomplishing anything.

Bill Dance is one of the world's most famous fishermen. Even people who don't fish know his name. According to (billdanceoutdoors.com), Bill Dance always planned to be a doctor like his father, grandfather, and three other generations before him. But after witnessing the aftermath of a horrific motorcycle accident, he decided to take a different path. Today, from his home and production studio in Collierville, Tennessee, Bill Dance oversees a fishing empire that includes his TV show, tackle endorsements, how-to seminars, his own magazine, and a series of popular blooper videos. The videos are hilarious!

These videos show outtakes from his fishing shows that were edited out of what was eventually aired on television. They show Bill Dance, the world's greatest fisherman getting his fishing lure caught in a tree, falling out of his boat, backing his truck over his rods and reels, getting hooks stuck in his fingers—you know, the stuff you and I do. That's the charm about Bill Dances' series of self-deprecating videos. I identify with him. I personally think those videos have done more to help build his fishing empire than hurt it. All of us who love to fish can relate to all the mistakes and blunders Bill Dance tends to make. He is the world's most famous fisherman and probably knows more about his craft than any human alive, but he still messes up from time to time.

Can I remind you that when you hear a song on the radio in which every beautiful note is sung with perfection, it was recorded in a studio after many takes (or I should say mistakes?). I love watching the outtakes following a movie. Getting to watch the mistakes that the actors made that were edited out of the finished product is very entertaining. The problem with real life is that there is no editing that takes place for you and me. We live our lives before our little part of the world, warts and all.

So what's the lesson? What can you and I learn from all of our mistakes and embarrassing moments? First of all, remember that God made you. He knows you, views you realistically, and loves you anyway.

God created us: "Then the LORD God formed a man from the dust of the ground and breathed into his nostrils the breath of life, and the man became a living being" (Genesis 2:7 NASB). God cares about us: "What is mankind that you are mindful of them, human beings that you care for them?" (Psalm 8:4 NIV). God understands us and is not shocked or surprised by our actions: "The LORD searches every heart and understands every desire and every thought" (1 Chronicles 28:9 NIV). Psalm 103:14 assures us, "For He knows how we are formed; He remembers that we are dust" (NIV). Our mistakes don't catch Him off guard, because He understands the limitations of our humanity.

Yes, God knows our weaknesses, but He also knows our potential. God has overseen the history of humankind and has witnessed countless mistakes. Others have failed and lived to tell about it. Your situation is not new.

Secondly, we must learn from our mistakes and failures. Winston Churchill is quoted as saying, "All men make mistakes, but only wise men learn from their mistakes." Through our mistakes, we gain knowledge. You must learn from your mistakes and embarrassing moments or they are forever wasted. I can honestly say that after every debacle, I have tried to walk away a wiser person. I refuse to allow the fear of making a mistake to keep me from accomplishing my dreams or reaching my goals. I have learned to accept those "What was I thinking?" moments as teachable moments.

Third, we must learn to laugh at ourselves. The Bible tells us that a cheerful heart is good medicine (Proverbs 17:22). Some of the funniest stuff is the stuff that happens to each of us in the process of living this thing called life.

People say that they would just die if certain things happened to them publicly. Well, I have learned firsthand that you do not die! The world didn't stop revolving simply because I messed up. If you can't learn to lighten up and laugh at yourself, you will become a very insecure, self-absorbed soul who will never attempt anything and be robbed of some real joy along life's journey.

Fourth, remember that mistakes are a sign of progress and growth. Conrad Hilton said that "Success seems to be connected with action. Successful people keep moving. They make mistakes, but they don't quit."

In Philippians 1:6, Paul wrote, "For I am confident of this very thing, that He who began a good work in you will perfect it until the day of Christ Jesus" (NASB). These words remind us that we are unfinished construction projects that God will not complete until He sees us face to face. Albert Einstein said, "Anyone who has never made a mistake has never tried anything new."

In the gospel of Matthew, you can read the story of how Peter stepped out of a boat during a storm and walked on water (Matthew 14:22–33). When he took his eyes off of Jesus, he began to sink. I'm not sure why we tend to focus on Peter's failure instead of his faith. The rest of the disciples sat in the boat. To my knowledge, Peter is the only person, other than Jesus, who walked on water, and that sounds pretty successful to me.

Rarely have any of us ever done anything to perfection. As a police officer, I successfully arrested robbers, purse snatchers, dope dealers, and even murders. I helped solve crimes and rescued people from dangerous situations. Not once do I recall everything being done to perfection. I did my best and gave my all, but for the most part, my performance was far from perfect.

Each of us is unique, and everyone has something to contribute. Since none of us are perfect, it should do us some good to be reminded that God has and will use imperfect people to accomplish great things. God is working on you. He is developing you. You and I are His perpetual construction projects.

You will make mistakes. Learn from those mistakes, but never allow the fear of making them to keep you from grabbing hold of your dreams. God has made you. You are unique, and He wants to use you in a great way—so please be willing to be used. Laugh off those silly mistakes. And in the meantime, if you find yourself afraid to act on your dreams simply because you are afraid of a possible mistake, take some advice from Barney Fife, and "Just nip it! Nip it in the bud!"

Questions for discussion and a call to action:

1. What dream would you attempt if you were not afraid to fail or be embarrassed? What action could you take today to move you toward that dream?

2. Which is the greater failure—to have made mistakes while attempting something noble or never to have made those attempts due to fear of failing?

3. What mistakes have you made that paid immediate dividends in lessons learned?

4. When Jesus said, "Therefore you shall be perfect, just as your Father in heaven is perfect" (Matthew 5:48 NKJV), does that mean He expected perfection from us?

5. How might knowing that God understands our limitations and frailties give us courage to risk great things for Him, even if failure looms as a possibility?

6. Remembering that God has and will use imperfect people to accomplish great things, ask Him right now to use you to bring glory to Him.

7. Memorize Philippians 4:13: "I can do all things through Him who strengthens me" (NASB).

To Serve and Protect
The Power of Our Service

In the city where I worked, the words "To serve and protect" were printed on the side of every marked police car. Every day that I worked for the police department, I was reminded of my mission. I was hired, trained, and paid to serve and protect the citizens of West Palm Beach, Florida. I took an oath. I made a promise.

Even at the age of twenty-one, I understood what it meant to protect something, but I had a lot to learn about actually serving a community.

I know that television sometimes makes police work look like a glamorous adventure, but in reality, the job is difficult, arduous, and dirty. People spit, bleed, and vomit on you. You wrestle drunks who don't bathe and people with diseases who try to bite you. There are the car accidents where you stand in the rain for hours, directing traffic, or the emotional heartache of having to notify people when their loved one dies. The paperwork is endless, because you must make a record of everything.

In the beginning, for me, learning to serve meant learning to be responsible. It meant being accountable to a higher authority and being found trustworthy. To serve and protect was about sacrifice and duty. I learned that serving was about being useful, and that in doing my job—my small part—I contributed to the greater good of the whole community. It was about putting others before me and serving while not caring who might get the credit.

Ann Landers said, "The true measure of a man is how he treats someone who can do him absolutely no good." I am still growing and maturing in my understanding of serving. But for a few moments, please allow me to share with you some of my observations about biblical serving.

Serving is not something that comes to us naturally. What comes naturally is to be served. We like receiving and taking and the temporary joy of getting, but the Bible teaches that there is no greater joy than the joy of serving—the joy of being a giver. Jesus said that it is "more blessed to give than to receive" (Acts 20:35 NASB).

Since serving is not a natural impulse, we have to be deliberate when thinking of who the object of service should be—that is, moving the emphasis from self to others. It involves replacing our thoughts and motives with those of Christ, because having the spirit of Christ is to have the spirit of a giver, not a taker.

God is a giver. According to James 1:17, He is the giver of "every good gift and every perfect gift" (NKJV). The most often quoted verse in the Bible reminds us that, "For God so loved this world that He gave ..." (John 3:16 NKJV).

Jesus is a giver. Jesus said, "Just as the Son of Man did not come to be served, but to serve, and to give his life as a ransom for many" (Matthew 20:28 NKJV). Jesus came into this world serving, giving, and contributing. The apostle Paul wrote in Philippians

2:5–8 that Jesus left all of the wonder of heaven and came to this earth, and when He did, He took on the form of a bond servant and became obedient even to the point of death.

God created us to serve and make a difference in the lives of others. According to Ephesians 2:10, "We are His workmanship, created in Christ Jesus for good works, which God prepared beforehand, that we should walk in them" (NKJV). You've heard the expression "built for speed." Well, we as God's children are built to serve. We were created for good works.

After Jesus washed the feet of the disciples, according to John 13:15, He turned to them and said, "For I gave you an example that you also should do as I did to you"(NASB). The example is one of humble service. Jesus wants His followers to be like Him—contributing, giving, and serving. We are never more like Jesus than when we are selflessly serving others.

I believe it's worth noting that before Jesus washed the feet of the disciples, He had "come forth from God and was going back to God" (John 13:3 NASB). You see, when you know who you are, where you came from, and where you are going, you can serve others with confidence.

Never lose sight of who you ultimately serve. "Serve wholeheartedly, as if you were serving the Lord, not people" (Ephesians 6:7 NIV). You are giving your best for the Master. "Whatever you do, work at it with all your heart, as working for the Lord, not for human masters" (Colossians 3:23 NIV). If you are trying to gain the accolades and appreciation of others and you wait for their praise, then you will be disappointed when what you are waiting for does not arrive.

Paul asked, "For am I now seeking the favor of men, or of God? Or am I striving to please men? If I were still trying to please men, I would not be a bond-servant of Christ" (Galatians 1:10 NASB). Regardless of what you do by way of your vocation or how much you love the work, all work gets old and tedious. You have to have the right perspective of your work or you will become discouraged. As Albert Schweitzer said, "I don't know what your destiny will be, but one thing I do know: the only ones among you who will be really happy are those who have sought and found how to serve."

God sees the value of your acts of service. He sees the value of what you are offering. Jesus, according to Matthew 10:42, recognized and rewarded even a simple cup of cold water given in His name. Since that is true, then God sees your contribution. Regardless of how great or small your contribution may be, it is valuable to Him. You may not even recognize the worth of your gift or kind deed, but God does. No one, with the exception of Jesus, was able to see the significance and value of the young boy's lunch that eventually fed thousands (John 6:8).

"Nobody made a greater mistake than he who did nothing because he could do only a little" (Edmund Burke). Every kind deed and every sacrifice will be rewarded. While others may never say thank you, your good work is noticed and it is noticed by the one who matters.

> Then the righteous will answer him, "Lord, when did we see you hungry and feed you, or thirsty and give you something to drink? When did we see you a stranger and invite you in, or needing clothes and clothe you? When did we see you sick or in prison and go to visit you?" The King will reply, "I tell you the truth, whatever you did for one of the least of these brothers of mine, you did for me." (Matthew 25:37–40 NASB)

Marian Wright Edelman said, "A lot of people are waiting for Martin Luther King or Mahatma Gandhi to come back—but they are gone. We are it. It is up to us. It is up to you."

Serve with a good attitude. The psalmist said to "Serve the LORD with gladness; Come before Him with joyful singing" (Psalm 100:2 NASB). The apostle Paul told us that "God loves a cheerful giver" (2 Corinthians 9:7 NASB). In the Sermon on the Mount, Jesus said, "If someone forces you to go one mile, go with him two miles" (Matthew 5:41 NIV). These verses speak about having a good attitude as we serve. They are about doing more than what is expected and not just doing the bare minimum in our service to others. As Albert Einstein said, "Only a life lived for others is a life worthwhile."

Serve now. Don't wait for ideal conditions or an audience to begin serving. Serve now. Solomon said, "Whoever watches the wind will not plant; whoever looks at the clouds will not reap" (Ecclesiastes 11:4). The New Living Translation puts it this way: "Farmers who wait for perfect weather never plant. If they watch every cloud, they never harvest." In the words of Marvin Wright Edelman, "It's time for greatness—not for greed. It's a time for idealism—not ideology. It is a time not just for compassionate words, but compassionate action."

Serve where you are. You don't have to travel to a foreign land to serve. Start where you are right now. God can use you to touch the lives of your coworkers. He wants to use you at home, school, or wherever He has placed you. Serve Him where you are today. I love what is written about David in Acts 13:36, where Luke said, "For David, after he had served the purpose of God in his own generation, fell asleep, and was laid among his fathers and underwent decay" (NASB). Just like David, you and I must serve in our generation. God can and will use us where He has placed us.

"How wonderful it is that nobody need wait a single moment before starting to improve the world" (Anne Frank).

Real greatness is found in serving. Jesus said, "Not so with you. Instead, whoever wants to become great among you must be your servant, and whoever wants to be first must be slave of all. For even the Son of Man did not come to be served, but to serve, and to give his life as a ransom for many" (Mark 10:43–45 NIV).

Real heroes serve! Greatness dons a towel and stoops to wash dirty feet. Greatness takes time for people who others would readily ignore. Greatness gives to those who are not capable of repayment. Greatness gets dirty helping the helpless. Greatness expends energy and spends money providing for the needs of neighbors. Greatness is apparent when the shirtsleeves are rolled up. In the words of Martin Luther King, Jr. "Everybody can be great … because anybody can serve. You don't have to have a college degree to serve. You don't have to make your subject and verb agree to serve. You only need a heart full of grace. A soul generated by love."

I heard about a police officer who took a routine vandalism report at an elementary school when he was interrupted by a little girl of about five years old. Looking the uniformed officer up and down, the little girl asked, "Are you a cop?"

The officer answered, "Yes," and continued writing his report.

The little girl said, "My mother said if I ever needed help, I should ask the police. Is that true?"

"Yes that's right," said the officer.

"Well, then," said the girl as she extended her foot toward him, "would you please tie my shoe?"

"A pessimist, they say, sees a glass of water as being half empty; an optimist sees the same glass as half full. But a giving person sees a glass of water and starts looking for someone who might be thirsty" (G. Donald Gale).

When a police officer begins his or her shift, he or she radios to headquarters to let dispatch know that he or she is "10-8," which is standard police code for "in service and ready for assignment." My prayer for you is that will start every day going "10-8," allowing the God who made you and is molding you to use you in His service.

Serve and protect: "Protect me, for I am devoted to you. Save me, for I serve you and trust you. You are my God" (Psalm 86:2 NLT).

Questions for discussion and a call to action:

1. Can you name some of the different types of people whom Jesus served?

2. What service or act of kindness was rendered to you in your moment of need?

3. What occasion did you have to serve someone during which you were edified and uplifted? Do you find that you are happier when you are serving or when you are being served?

4. Read Philippians 2:5–8. When Paul decreed, "Have this attitude in yourselves which was also in Christ Jesus" (v. 5 NASB), did it sound like something he considered as optional in a Christian's life? If an attitude of serving doesn't come easily for you, what in Paul's description of Jesus' own attitude could help you personally in developing this quality?

5. What action could you take today—right now—to serve someone?

6. Memorize Matthew 20:28: "Just as the Son of Man did not come to be served, but to serve, and to give His life as a ransom for many."

5

Shoot—Don't Shoot
The Power of Our Choices

There is great power in the choices that you and I make. For a police officer, the right decision can save an innocent life, and the wrong decision can take one.

One training exercise that many law enforcement agencies have used effectively to help prepare officers for split-second decisions is a film called *Shoot or Don't Shoot.* In West Palm, officers would report to the indoor firing range and load their guns with blanks. Down range, on the screen in front of the officers, the film depicts various situations in which officers routinely find themselves, such as traffic stops, bank alarms, and domestic disturbances. These scenarios are shown from the perspective of the officer and have dangerous elements placed within each situation that would force the officer to make a decision either to shoot or not to shoot.

Brent Wittmeier, in an article written for the *Edmonton Journal* entitled "Training Police to Confront Hostile Situations," said that

A police officer has about 1.7 seconds to decide to use deadly force to end a hostile situation. By the time an officer is ready to pull the trigger, he or she may have already been shot. So much is at stake in those 1.7 seconds. Officers may face years of investigations, lawsuits, damaged reputations and regrets. After a shooting, it's often difficult to just explain what happened or why, let alone recount crucial small details. And officers aren't allowed to talk about the incident with their peers in case they damage the investigation.

One point seven seconds is a minuscule amount of time. When faced with a life-or-death decision, you must make sure those seconds count. I realize that you may not make life-and-death decisions in a limited amount of time on a daily basis, but you are making decisions and choices that affect your life and the lives of others.

For all of us, life is a series of choices. What we are today represents the decisions and choices of our yesterdays. What we become in the future will be determined by the choices that we make today. It was Albert Einstein who defined insanity as "doing the same thing over and over again and expecting different results." If you want to change the direction of your life for the better, then start making better choices.

It was amazing how so few of the men, women, and teenagers I arrested ever actually owned up, confessed, or admitted that they had made some very poor choices. Most were more upset about being caught than actually committing a crime. Rarely was it their fault.

I realize that some people have inherited difficult circumstances or have heartache in their lives that they never wanted or asked for but is theirs nonetheless. Maybe they were born into an evil environment and abused by people who should have loved and cared for them. It's as though they were born with two strikes already against them. Some of the finest people I know have come out of these kinds of circumstances and are living successful lives. They have stopped the cycle of abuse and poverty in their generation. The Bible teaches, "To whom much is given, from him much will be required" (Luke 12:48 KJV).

These folks were not given much, but they took what few opportunities and gifts they received, invested the few resources they were given, and then climbed higher than many who were born into privilege and affluence. Much of their success had everything to do with their choices. These may have not chosen their lot in life, but they did choose how they would respond. They chose their attitudes toward their circumstances—whether they would be victims or victors.

Many people blame their lives, health, or circumstances on anything and everything other than their poor choices. It's their parents' fault, the government's fault, or the church's fault. My dad used to say, "If we could kick the person most responsible for our problems, we wouldn't be able to sit down for a week!"

Jails and prisons are filled with men and women who just made poor choices. They might blame the system, the police, or their lawyers, but if they are honest about the evaluation of their lives, they will admit that they made choices that directed them down a path of destruction.

Psalm 36:4 says, "He plans wickedness upon his bed; he sets himself on a path that is not good; he does not despise evil" (NASB). He "sets himself on a path." Even before they robbed a bank or burglarized a home, they made choices. They made plans. Maybe it was to experiment with drugs, and that addiction brought them to yet another poor choice. At any moment, they could have chosen different paths for their lives. At any moment, they could have chosen to reach out and get some help for their addiction. At any moment, they could have stopped an immoral behavior. But they chose not to stop.

That is the great dilemma within our nation today. People complain constantly about their plight in life and act as though they have no control over its direction. They see themselves as helpless victims who are unable to ever climb out of despair. They wait for someone else to step in and make changes only they can make. Les Brown said, "We must look for ways to be an active force in our own lives. We must take charge of our own destinies, design a life of substance and truly begin to live our dreams."

I was watching an episode of *COPS* in which one of the police officers being interviewed at the beginning of a segment mentioned how he had been in some trouble as a teenager. He explained how that experience changed him. He said, "I decided then and there that I wanted to be on the right side of the law and not on the wrong side." Apparently the kindness and professionalism of his arresting officer caused him to want to be like that man one day. He made a choice and that choice changed his life. He obviously had to make some new friends, pursue higher education, and live in such a way that he would one day qualify for entrance into a police academy. He accomplished his goal. He made a choice that was followed by a series of other choices that brought him to that point in his life.

One evening, while patrolling the south end of West Palm Beach, Florida, I was dispatched to a home in reference to an injured person. The paramedics had also been summoned, but I was the first to arrive. "Injured person" was an understatement. As I pulled into the driveway, I saw a man calmly sitting in his front yard with a red towel wrapped around his arm. It didn't take long to figure out the towel was soaked in blood and that the injured man probably didn't have long to live. Another officer and I kept pressure in the right places to slow the loss of blood until the ambulance arrived. Later, a helicopter was flown in, and the man was air lifted from one hospital to another that specialized in reattaching severed limbs.

As you can imagine, my first question was, "What happened here?" I discovered that this man and his wife had been having a petty disagreement. As they argued, he became so angry that he punched a window in their bedroom, shattering glass out into the back yard. But when he pulled his arm back through the window, he caught it on the jagged glass and severed it just above the elbow. That was a choice I am sure he regretted. If he had just thought through his actions and tried to calm his anger, the outcome might have been entirely different. If he had it to do all over again, I am sure he would have made different choices. But isn't that true for all of us? We have all made choices that we regret. We all wish we could get a second chance.

I know you have heard this before, but we must learn from our mistakes and poor choices or they are wasted. With God's help, we make better choices. Even if we have made poor choices in the past, we shouldn't feel trapped or helpless, because we can make better choices—good choices—and in doing so, we will change the path of our lives.

What are some of the lessons we learn when it comes to the power of our choices? First is that the choices and decisions we make will shape our lives. The words of Eleanor Roosevelt ring true:

"One's philosophy is not best expressed in words. It is expressed in the choices one makes. In the long run, we shape our lives and we shape ourselves. The process never ends until we die. And the choices we make are ultimately our responsibility."

When God spoke to the people of Israel through Moses, He challenged them to think about the consequences of their choices:

Now what I am commanding you today is not too difficult for you or beyond your reach. It is not up in heaven, so that you have to ask, "Who will ascend into heaven to get it and proclaim it to us so we may obey it?" Nor is it beyond the sea, so that you have to ask, "Who will cross the sea to get it and proclaim it to us so we may obey it?" No, the word is very near you; it is in your mouth and in your heart so you may obey it. See, I set before you today life and prosperity, death and destruction. For I command you today to love the LORD your God, to walk in obedience to him, and to keep his commands, decrees and laws; then you will live and increase, and the LORD your God will bless you in the land you are entering to possess. But if your heart turns away and you are not obedient, and if you are drawn away to bow down to other gods and worship them, I declare to you this day that you will certainly be destroyed. You will not live long in the land you are crossing the Jordan to enter and possess. This day I call the heavens and the earth as witnesses against you that I have set before you life and death, blessings and curses. Now choose life, so that you and your children may live and that you may love the LORD your God, listen to his voice, and hold fast to him. For the LORD is your life, and he will give you many years in the land he swore to give to your fathers, Abraham, Isaac and Jacob. (Deuteronomy 30:11–20 NIV)

Second, if you do not make a positive decision about the direction of your life, then someone else may make a negative decision for you. Former President Ronald Reagan once had an aunt who took him to a cobbler for a pair of new shoes. The cobbler asked young Reagan, "Do you want square toes or round toes?" Unable to decide, Reagan didn't answer, so the cobbler gave him a few days. Several days later, the cobbler saw Reagan on the street and asked him again what kind of toes he wanted on his shoes. Reagan still couldn't decide, so the shoemaker replied, "Well, come by in a couple of days. Your shoes will be ready." When the future president did so, he found one square-toed and one round-toed shoe! "This will teach you to never let people make decisions for you," the cobbler said to his indecisive customer.

"I learned right then and there," Reagan said later, "if you don't make your own decisions, someone else will" (*Today in the Word*, MBI, August, 1991, 16).

Third, your choices (good and bad) not only affect you, but also others. They may affect your parents, spouse, children, or even grandchildren. Your choices will reach into the next generation. Psalm 78:4–7 says that our choices will touch "a generation to come."

When the conquest of Canaan was concluded and Joshua gave parting words to the fledgling nation of Israel, his admonition acknowledged the far-reaching implications of one's choices.

Now therefore fear the Lord and serve Him in sincerity and truth; and put away the gods which your fathers served beyond the River and in Egypt, and serve the Lord. If it is disagreeable in your sight to serve the Lord, choose for yourselves today whom you will serve; whether the gods which your fathers served which were beyond the River, or the gods of the Amorites in whose land you are living; but as for me and my house, we will serve the Lord. (Joshua 24:14–15 NASB)

Joshua, no doubt, was present when Moses gave his own farewell address, (Deuteronomy 30:11–20). Inspired by God, Moses anticipated that his fellow Israelites would make wrong choices that would inevitably bring about their downfall. Joshua was determined that would not happen on his watch, particularly in reference to his own family. Even if the rest of Israel should choose to go astray, Joshua was determined that he "and his house" would serve the Lord. He understood the wisdom of his mentor's advice to "teach [God's word] diligently to your sons, and shall talk of them when you sit in your house, and when you walk by the way, and when you lie down, and when you rise up" (Deuteronomy 6:7 NASB). Joshua realized that apostasy was just one generation away, and prevention required a concentrated effort to pass his faith down to his own children so that they, in turn, would do the same. Good choices are dependent upon good teaching.

Remember that our lives reflect the constant practice of the law of the harvest. It is the lesson of sowing and reaping. People will get out of life what they put into it. We will redeem what we have invested. The Bible claims in Galatians 6:7, "Don't be deceived, God is not mocked, for whatever a man sows, this he will also reap" (NASB).

The law of the harvest is simply this: If you plant (or sow) a kernel of corn, then you will grow (or reap) a stalk of corn. You cannot sow corn and reap green beans. You always get back the kind that you plant. You will always get back more than you planted, and you have to be patient when waiting for the harvest, because we reap later than we sow.

Like the law of gravity, the law of the harvest is a law. You cannot alter or change this law. You will get out of your life what you invest in it. This law is unbiased; the results can be good as well as bad. If you sow good things, then you will reap a good harvest, and if you sow evil things, then you will reap disaster! That is the law of the harvest. It is unchangeable and undeniable, but it is the law, and the choices you make determine how that law will affect your life.

The Bible claims in Numbers 32:23 that "your sin will find you out." Notice it does not say that sin "may find you out" but that it "will find you out." When we live our lives on a path of destruction, why should we be surprised when we are destroyed?

One evening, a man was working late in his office in the downtown area. As he got up from his desk to stretch his legs and get a cup of coffee, he happened to look out his office window and witness a crime being committed. At the rear door of a building adjacent to his office complex, he could see what appeared to be a burglary in progress. From his vantage point, he could see a man wearing a hat and gloves, chiseling away at the rear door of an oriental carpet business. When the call was dispatched from headquarters, I happened to be just a few blocks away. I parked my police car and crept through an alley right up behind the man. He wasn't wearing a hat but a ski mask! He wore gloves to cover his fingerprints, and with a hammer in one hand and a chisel in the other, he was making so much noise trying to get the hinges off the back door of that business that he never heard me coming.

He jumped a mile high when I pointed my gun at him and told him to get down on the ground.

It turns out that this man owned a successful business of his own and had been in that carpet store earlier the same day with his wife and decided that he didn't want to pay for an oriental carpet; he would just steal it instead. It was a choice he would regret. That day, the man sowed bad seed and reaped a bad harvest. He deliberately disobeyed the law of our city and one of God's laws—"Thou shall not steal"—and he reaped the consequences.

That night, something was stolen—but not from a carpet business. Something was stolen from the life of the man who chose to sow the wrong kind of seed. First, his freedom was stolen, because I put him in jail. Then his reputation was stolen. As if that were not enough, his family's trust and admiration were taken from him as well.

When you understand the law of the harvest, then you can practice it to your advantage every day. You can invest good things and be repaid with an abundance of good things. Invest the right kind of attitude. Invest the right kind of influence. Invest with the right kind of motives.

Finally, know that you *can* change the path of your life! That is great news! God is a God of second chances, and you don't have to live a defeated life based solely on your past choices. You can make present choices that can change your future.

There were several in the Corinth church who made a conscious decision to change the course of their lives. They were involved in all kinds of sexually immorality. They were thieves, greedy, drunkards, revilers, and swindlers. But they didn't stay that way. Paul emphasized, "And such were some of you. But you were washed, you were sanctified, you were justified in the name of the

Lord Jesus Christ and by the Spirit of our God" (1 Corinthians 6:11 NASB). Previous choices led to sinful lifestyles, but they didn't have to remain on that destructive course. The decision to cease those behaviors and be obedient to the gospel changed their futures from destruction to sanctification and justification.

Be honest with yourself. Could it be that the harvest of your life stinks because you have sowed the wrong kind of seed? If so, then change! Turn your life around before it is too late, and start sowing the right kind of seed. It is all about the choices you make. You will probably never have to decide whether or not to pull the trigger of a gun on a criminal, but the decisions you make still have life-and-death implications, physically and spiritually speaking.

If you have not taken care of yourself physically, then change and do the kind of things that will keep the one body you have been given by God healthy. If you have made some poor choices in your relationships, then change, and start making better dating choices. Start choosing better quality people to spend time with, knowing that "bad company corrupts good character" (1 Corinthians 15:33 NIV). If you have filled your mind with worldly material and impure thoughts, then change. Meditate instead on the Word of God. Choose life and prosperity over death and destruction. Choose to serve God rather than the gods in the land around you. Your choices have the power to direct your future. Resolve to make the right ones!

Questions for discussion and a call to action:

1. For better or worse, how have you witnessed the law of the harvest working in your life?
2. What choices have you made that set you on a different path?
3. How have you been affected by the choices of your parents and grandparents? How have your own children or grandchildren been affected by your choices?
4. How does the fact that God is a God of a second chances give you hope?
5. What seed do you need to sow today in order to have a great harvest tomorrow?
6. Memorize Galatians 6:9: "Let us not become weary in doing good, for at the proper time we will reap a harvest if we do not give up."

Live by a Code
The Power of God's Word

From January 17 through March 14, 1977, I was privileged to be one of thirty recruits attending the police academy at the Palm Beach Junior College Criminal Justice Institute. We were Basic Recruit Class #13, and I turned twenty-one the day before graduation.

One of the first (and I believe one of most important) concepts that we were taught at the very beginning of that police academy was that we were expected to live by a code. All recruits were given a copy of the *Law Enforcement Code of Ethics* to be placed at the very front of our academy course notebooks.

According to the Encarta Dictionary, a code is "a system of accepted laws and regulations that govern procedure or behavior in particular circumstances or within a particular profession." The *Law Enforcement Code of Ethics* describes a group of individuals who should be as concerned about their private conduct as they are about their professional conduct. There was an expectation that police officers would conduct themselves by a high standard that would govern their behavior and understand that they were to live as though they would be held accountable.

Did you know that God wants all of us to live by a code? It's true. God's desire for all humankind is that we aspire to a higher standard. The standard that I am speaking about applies to more than just the law enforcement community. This code, the Bible, is for all people.

Because God is our Creator, He knows what is best for us. He not only created our bodies, but also our minds, hearts, and souls. Our Creator wants what is best for us eternally. He even knows what standards, principles, and rules will protect, bless, and fulfill us! Therefore, He put these into His code. A code can be good, but His code is optimal. Any good code written by humans contains some ideas from God's optimal code.

God's code, the Bible, provides boundaries for our health and safety. It gives direction. It is a road map to heaven and a success manual for life. As a matter of fact, it contains everything necessary for *"life and godliness"* (2 Peter 1:3).

God challenged the people of ancient Israel when they failed to live up to the code He had given them: "And you will know that I am the LORD, for you have not followed my decrees or kept my laws but have conformed to the standards of the nations around you" (Ezekiel 11:12 NIV). The Israelites lowered the bar. They ignored God's higher code, settled for the lesser pagan standard, and paid the price.

There are several reasons you should want to live your life based on the Bible, God's great code for all humanity. First, God's code is divinely inspired. In 2 Timothy 3:16–17, Paul wrote to young Timothy and said that "All Scripture is inspired by God and profitable for teaching, for reproof, for correction, for training in righteousness; so that the man of God may be adequate, equipped for every good work" (NASB).

The Bible, which includes both the Old and New Testaments, is the inspired and revealed Word of God. While it comes to us through the pens of human writers, the real source was the Spirit of God Himself. "Knowing this first of all, that no prophecy of Scripture comes from someone's own interpretation. For no prophecy was ever produced by the will of man, but men spoke from God as they were carried along by the Holy Spirit" (2 Peter 1:20–21 ESV).

When we read from this code, we hear from a being that knows *all* things. Isaiah asked rhetorically, "Who has directed the Spirit of the LORD, or as His counselor has informed Him? With whom did He consult and who gave Him understanding? And who taught Him in the path of justice and taught Him knowledge and informed Him of the way of understanding?" (Isaiah 40:13–14 NASB). God doesn't need anyone to teach Him anything, because all knowledge proceeds from Him. You can be certain that the words you read come from a person who knows what He is talking about. The Bible is the first and final authority by which God wants all people to live.

Second, God's code distinguishes right from wrong. I love Psalm 119:128 in the New Living Translation: "Each of your commandments is right. That is why I hate every false way."

I was reminded that people still do possess a conscience and that they can know right from wrong. While on patrol one evening, I was stopped at an intersection in downtown West Palm Beach when a man in his mid-twenties jumped into the back of my police car and yelled, "I give up; arrest me!"

After pulling this character back out of my police car and searching him, I discovered that there was, indeed, a warrant out for his arrest. It was the easiest arrest I ever made! On the way to the police department, I asked him what caused him to surrender. His answer stunned me. He said, "Every time I hear a siren or see a police car driving in my direction, every time I see a policeman walking into a restaurant where I am eating, I just know that they are coming for me. I am tired of living while looking back over my shoulder. I just wanted to get this over with and clear my mind and get my life back." This young man knew, deep down, that he was living contrary to the life God wanted for him. He still had a conscience. He knew right from wrong, and he knew he was living wrong. Jesus said, "The truth will set you free" (John 8:32). While it is true that this man went to jail because of his crime, he was finally free, and his conscience was clear.

The writer of Hebrews, in speaking of the elementary truths of God's Word, made this observation: "Anyone who lives on milk, being still an infant, is not acquainted with the teaching about righteousness. But solid food is for the mature, who by constant use have trained themselves to distinguish good from evil" (Hebrews 5:13–14 NIV). The Word of God allows one to accurately discern between what is right and wrong.

Third, God's code will last forever. Listen to the promise in Isaiah 40:8: "The grass withers, the flower fades, but the word of our God stands forever" (NKJV). I love 1 Peter 1:25: "…'but the word of the Lord endures forever.' And this is the word that was preached to you" (NIV).

Many codes appeared in history and then disappeared. For example, The Code of Hammurabi is a well-preserved ancient code of law created around 1790 BC in ancient Babylon. It was enacted by the sixth Babylonian king, Hammurabi. One nearly complete example of the code survives today and is kept on display at the Louvre in Paris, France. Although many efforts have been made throughout history to destroy the Scriptures they have all failed. The Bible, God's Code, will stand the test of time and endure forever.

Fourth, God's code is trustworthy. The Bible states in 1 Kings 8:56, "Praise be to the LORD, who has given rest to His people Israel just as He promised. Not one word has failed of all the good promises He gave through His servant Moses" (NIV). In Matthew 5:18, Jesus said, "I tell you the truth, until heaven and earth disappear, not the smallest letter, not the least stroke of a pen, will by any means disappear from the Law until everything is accomplished" (NIV).

The author of this code is not only omniscient, but also incapable of lying (Titus 1:2, Hebrews 6:18). His nature prevents Him from speaking anything but truth. Because of His intense love for us, we can expect Him to tell us the truth, even when it hurts or when it may be something we really don't want to hear. Combine all three of those characteristics—that God is all-knowing, all-loving, and always truthful—and you can come to some hard and fast conclusions. You can trust God's Word and know for certain that God will keep His promises. God's code is trustworthy. God will do what He said He will do!

Fifth, God's code is the path to prosperity and success. I'm greatly encouraged by what God told Joshua following the death of Moses:

Be strong and courageous, because you will lead these people to inherit the land I swore to their forefathers to give them. Be strong and very courageous. Be careful to obey all the law my servant Moses gave you; do not turn from it to the right or to the left, that you may be successful wherever you go. Do not let this Book of the Law depart from your mouth; meditate on it day and night, so that you may be careful to do everything written in it. Then you will be prosperous and successful. Have I not commanded you? Be strong and courageous. Do not be terrified; do not be discouraged, for the LORD your God will be with you wherever you go. (Joshua 1:6–9 NIV)

Real success is achieved by being obedient to God's code for your life. Listen to Psalm 1:1–3 NIV:

Blessed is the one who does not walk in step with the wicked or stand in the way that sinners take or sit in the company of mockers, but whose delight is in the law of the LORD, and who meditates on his law day and night. That person is like a tree planted by streams of water, which yields its fruit in season and whose leaf does not wither—whatever they do prospers.

Let me reiterate that I said *real* success. I think it is worthwhile to prepare you for the right kind of expectations. The prosperity and success that God promises may not come in the same form as the world views those things. True success in God's eyes really has little to do with how much wealth a person has. If you follow His code and if you believe the author of that code knows everything, never lies to you, and loves you so much that He wants only what is best for you, then you'll have no trouble leaving the details of that prosperity and success in His hands.

Finally, God's code is your GPS system for life. In Proverbs 6:23 NIV, we are told, "For these commands are a lamp, this teaching is a light, and the corrections of discipline are the way to life." David said in Psalm 119:105 NIV, "Your word is a lamp to my feet and a light for my path."

GPS stands for *global positioning system*. It is a system designed for navigation. The Bible is our GPS—our navigation system for living. It sets before us worthy goals to achieve. It gives heaven as our destination and then instructs us how to navigate this life successfully so that we might arrive safely at that destination. "He who keeps the commandment keeps his soul, but he who is careless of conduct will die" (Proverbs 19:16 NASB). If we will keep God's word, God's word will keep us from harm.

When you discover God's code for your life and really desire to live according to that code, then some changes will take place from the inside out. No one can force you to change. The police can enforce the law, but they cannot make anyone obey the law who doesn't want to obey.

According to 2 Chronicles 34, Josiah was only eight years old when he became king, and he died in battle around the age of thirty-nine. Josiah's father and grandfather were evil rulers. But Josiah followed a different path, and as a result, he left a very different legacy. The Bible tells us that "Josiah removed all the detestable idols from all the territory belonging to the Israelites, and he had all who were present in Israel serve the LORD their God. As long as he lived, they did not fail to follow the LORD, the God of their fathers" (2 Chronicles 34:33 NIV).

What made the difference in the character—and consequently, the heritage—of Josiah? When Josiah was about twenty-four and was in the process of cleaning up "the temple of the LORD," apparently, "Hilkiah the priest found the Book of the Law of the LORD that had been given through Moses. Hilkiah said to

Shaphan the secretary, 'I have found the Book of the Law in the temple of the LORD.' He gave it to Shaphan." Shaphan then read the Book of the Law to Josiah, and Josiah grieved, because the people of Israel were not living according to the code. Josiah set out to make some changes to get his nation up to code. It was a discovery that changed the life and legacy of Josiah!

Josiah's reform was a great accomplishment. Second Kings 23:25 tells us that "Neither before nor after Josiah was there a king like him who turned to the Lord as he did—with all his heart and with all his soul and with all his strength, in accordance with all the Law of Moses." I wish this had a happy ending for Josiah's people. But the very next verse reads, "Nevertheless, the LORD did not turn away from the heat of his fierce anger, which burned against Judah because of all that Manasseh had done to provoke him to anger" (2 Kings 23:26 NIV). Despite his courageous efforts, Josiah did not succeed in changing people's hearts. When I read of all the things he did to reform his nation, I realize that they all happened because he made them happen.

Josiah was the one who trembled at the Word of God. He was the one who sought the counsel of godly people and called everyone together to renew the covenant. He was the one who personally supervised the destruction of all the idolatry and ordered the people to celebrate a Passover such as had not been seen since the days of the Judges. What Josiah failed to do was change the heart of the nation. Only God's Word has the power to transform a life and a nation.

It is my prayer that you will read God's powerful code, the Bible, meditate on it, and then do the things that God has directed. It will be as a light to your path. It will help you navigate your life's journey and then arrive at our final destination safely. Based on the authority of God's Word, I can make this promise: when you choose to live by God's code, you will have selected a path to real, lasting happiness, and you will discover the true riches of this life and the next.

Questions for discussion and a call to action:

1. What are the results of a nation ignoring God's Word? In what ways can you observe moral decay going on in America that could have been avoided had God's will been heeded and obeyed?
2. God told Joshua that obedience to His words would bring prosperity and success. How have you seen this truth lived out in your life?
3. What Scripture has been a continual source of inspiration for you?
4. What would your life be like if the Word of God were not a part of it?
5. Ask God to help you think of some unique and inventive ways to share and teach God's Word to others.
6. Memorize Psalm 119:105: "Your word is a lamp to my feet and a light for my path."

Law Enforcement Code of Ethics

As a Law Enforcement Officer, my fundamental duty is to serve mankind; to safeguard lives and property; to protect the innocent against deception, the weak against oppression or intimidation, and the peaceful against violence or disorder; and to respect the Constitutional rights of all persons to liberty, equality and justice.

I will keep my private life unsullied as an example to all; maintain courageous calm in the face of danger, scorn or ridicule; develop self-restraint; and be constantly mindful of the welfare of others. Honest in thought and deed in both my personal and official life, I will be exemplary in obeying the laws of the land and the regulations of my department. Whatever I see or hear of a confidential nature or that is confided to me in my official capacity will be kept ever secret unless revelation is necessary in the performance of my duty.

I will never act officiously or permit personal feelings, prejudices, animosities or friendships to influence my decisions. With no compromise for crime and with relentless prosecution of criminal, I will enforce the law courteously and appropriately without fear or favor, malice or ill will, never employing unnecessary force or violence and never accepting gratuities.

I recognize the badge of my office as a symbol of public faith, and I accept it as a public trust to be held so long as I am true to the ethics of the police service. I will constantly strive to achieve these objectives and ideals, dedicating myself before God to my chosen profession … law enforcement.

7

Blessed Are the Peace Officers
The Power of a Self-Controlled Life

I n many law enforcement communities, the phrase "police officer" is used interchangeably with "peace officer." An officer of the law keeps or maintains the peace within his or her jurisdiction.

Did you know that the office of sheriff came down to us from the common law of England? Dating from the times of King Alfred (tenth-century England), the term *sheriff* evolved from the Old English term *shire reeve*. A sheriff was a royal official responsible for keeping the peace (a *reeve*) throughout a shire or county on behalf of the king. (Robin Hood, a character in English folklore, was sought by the Sheriff of Nottinghamshire.)

When the Old West was confronted with serious issues of crime, disorder, and violence, the pioneers turned to members of their communities to enforce order. With a multi-century background and history, the office of sheriff was a natural addition in this setting. The sheriff was the peace officer, and the judge was known as the justice of the peace.

Jesus is called the Prince of Peace in Isaiah 9:6. And in Proverbs 3:17, Solomon wrote that all of the paths of wisdom lead to peace. God exhorts us in Psalm 34:14 to "depart from evil and do good; seek peace and pursue it" (NKJV). All of us should strive to become officers of peace.

There is a difference between peacekeeping and peacemaking. A peacekeeper is someone who attempts to prevent fights, violence and disputes. A peacemaker is someone who endeavors to get a fight or dispute under control once they do occur. Even with that distinction, the police officer does both.

Peacekeeping means keeping people from attacking each other by putting some kind of barrier between them. As a young man, my father, while serving in the United States Army, was wounded fighting in Korea so that peace would come to that region. Peace came in the form of a barrier called the 38th parallel. Today, there is still animosity between South and North Korea. Even while I write these words, the United States military stands guard at the 38th parallel to maintain or keep the peace.

Peacemaking is the process of forging a resolution between disputing parties. It takes more than a peace accord to bring peace to a fragile situation. For any long-term peace, there must be peace building. There must be the progression of building relationships and reconciling differences between the warring factions.

Peace officers have a few characteristics. They understand that they cannot give away something they themselves do not possess. There is a progression to this peace process. If you are going to be a peace-keeper, peace-maker, peace-builder, and peace officer, then there must be peace in your own life. James said, "And the seed whose fruit is righteousness is sown in peace by those who make peace" (James 3:18 NASB).

First and foremost, make peace with God yourself. "Therefore being justified by faith, we have peace with God through our Lord Jesus Christ … For if while we were enemies we were reconciled to God through the death of His Son, much more, having been reconciled, we shall be saved by His life" (Romans 5:1, 10 NASB). Until you have personally dealt with the problem of sin in your own life, your status with God is as His enemy.

To be reconciled means to "make friends again." Without reconciliation to God, you are not in any position to move to the next step. This involves making contact with the blood of Jesus (Romans 5:9) in the death of Jesus (Romans 5:10, 6:3–4) so that you can have a peace with God through Jesus (5:1, 11). It is a peace "which transcends all understanding" (Philippians 4:7). David wrote in his journal, "I will lie down and sleep in peace, for you alone, O Lord, make me dwell in safety" (Psalm 4:8 NIV).

Once peace is established between you and God, then you can move to help others make peace with God, too. Watch how Paul explained how he, along with the other apostles, made the transition from reconciled to reconcilers.

Now all these things are from God, who reconciled us to Himself through Christ and gave us the ministry of reconciliation, namely, that God was in Christ reconciling the world to Himself, not counting their trespasses against them, and He has committed to us the word of reconciliation. Therefore, we are ambassadors for Christ, as though God were making an appeal through us; we beg you on behalf of Christ, be reconciled to God. (2 Corinthians 5:18–20 NASB)

We should follow their lead and become peace ambassadors, helping others be at peace with God, since we ourselves have received peace from God.

With peace established between us and God, there is then a basis for seeking peace with one another. "If it is possible, as far as it depends on you, live at peace with everyone" (Roman 12:18 NIV). It would be difficult for us to fully comprehend the level of animosity that has existed through time between Jews and Gentiles. When the Jew offered his usual morning prayer, he would first thank God that he was not made a Gentile. Yet one of the things accomplished by the cross of Christ was the ability to finally bridge the gap between the two warring parties.

Speaking to Gentiles, Paul (from the vantage point of a Jew) claimed,

> Remember that you were at that time separated from Christ, excluded from the commonwealth of Israel and strangers to the covenants of promise, having no hope and without God in the world. But now in Christ Jesus you who once were far off have been brought near by the blood of Christ. For He himself is our peace, who has made us both one and has broken down in his flesh the dividing wall of hostility by abolishing the law of commandments expressed in ordinances, that he might create in himself one new man in place of the two, so making peace. (Ephesians 2:12–15 NASB)

The same cross that made it possible for Jew and Gentile to experience peace can reconcile enemies on any level.

A peace officer is at peace in his or her own life. He or she makes peace with God and helps others do the same. Then, with his or her best efforts, he or she makes peace with others and helps them reconcile with their own enemies.

Peace officers practice self-control. When you practice self-control, your life will be built up and fortified. There will be a peace within and calm without.

If you lack self-control, then your life will be dismantled. Solomon said, "Like a city that is broken into and without walls is a man who has no control over his spirit" (Proverbs 25:28 NASB). A city without walls is vulnerable to attack and destruction. None of us will ever be truly successful in this life until we learn the lesson of self-control. I have learned this about self-control: school is never out! Just when you seem to get one area of your life under control, you see weakness in another area. It is an ongoing battle—but one worth fighting.

Paul wrote, "All things are lawful for me, but not all things are profitable. All things are lawful for me, but I will not be mastered by anything" (1 Corinthians 6:12 NASB). Have you allowed anything to have control over you?

Self-control is getting up at a certain time because you have a responsibility to an employer. Lack of self-control is staying in bed and then arriving late to work. Self-control is guarding your tongue. Lack of self-control is saying whatever comes into your head. Self-control is having a budget. Lack of self-control is buying whatever you want and running up credit card debt. You get the idea. One can have a lack of control in eating or the consumption of alcohol.

If there is a lack of control in your life, then you are vulnerable to attack and destruction. If something else is your master, then you will never reach the full potential that God has placed within you. You will not be at peace or be a peacemaker.

If you work just one day in the field of law enforcement, you will witness the destruction of countless lives due to lack of self-control. It's not uncommon for people to lose their temper and strike out at another with their fists or a car. The lack of self-control with alcohol creates accidents, DUI arrests, and deaths. Laziness and a lack of any ambition create robberies, shopliftings, and purse snatches. The list is endless. City jails and prisons are filled with men and women who never learned the lesson of self-control.

If you want to fulfill the God-given potential of your life, develop some self-control. Be a self-starter. Be a self-motivator. Ask God to help you, and then get going! Quit making excuses for your laziness and immaturity. You need to take charge of your life and overcome habits and addictions that hold you back from being all that God wants you to be. God encourages us in 1 Peter 5:8 to "Be self-controlled and alert. Your enemy the devil prowls around like a roaring lion looking for someone to devour."

Peace officers move toward, not away, from the conflict. One of the most graphic pictures that many Americans will always have imprinted onto their memories of September 11, 2001 in New York City is the picture of first responders, police officers, fireman, and rescue workers running into buildings that thousands were trying to run out of and away from. They were trained, like I was, to move toward the conflict and not away from it. They put themselves in harm's way, and many gave the ultimate sacrifice.

We know that courage is not the absence of fear. You can be afraid and still act courageously. It's not wrong to be afraid; it's natural. What is wrong and unnatural is to allow your fears to keep you away from difficult situations and circumstances that demand your presence. Much of what is wrong today in our relationships could simply be corrected if people would quit ignoring, avoiding, and dodging difficult circumstances and problems and start moving toward them.

When a fellow police officer is down, involved in an accident, or calls for help, no matter where you are or what you are doing, you immediately move toward the conflict. It does not matter the color of her skin, his political preference, or even if you like the person or not; you try to be the first one there to help. All police departments have this in common. I don't care if the department has five or five hundred employees; each member is part of the family, and that is what officers do—they go. They cover each other and watch each other's backs, and if there is a man or woman in the family who is hesitant to do that, then he or she needs to find another occupation.

When I worked for West Palm Beach Police Department, I had many opportunities to cover fellow officers who asked for backup or some kind of assistance. One particular afternoon, a fellow police officer was involved in a struggle with two individuals who were attempting to take his weapon away. He was fighting for his life, so you can imagine how stressed and panicked his voice sounded coming across the police radio. I bolted toward him. As safe and as fast as I could drive, I moved toward the conflict.

As long as I live, I will never forget the sight or the feeling that I had that day as I watched a fellow officer driving in the opposite direction. He was moving away from the fight at a casual rate of speed. It's not surprising that he never made it through his probation period and was encouraged to seek employment elsewhere. I understand that the other officer was afraid. I was afraid, and so were others—but that didn't keep us from traveling as fast as we could toward the conflict so that we could help the situation and be a part of the solution.

Many people live their lives moving away from conflict, heartache, and problems, thinking they are keeping the peace in the process. They act as though in ignoring them or denying problems, they will vanish; but instead, problems fester, and conflicts escalate. Move toward the conflicts and not away from them. Rarely will a problem solve itself or a conflict resolve itself. Real peace can't exist until sin is addressed.

Wasn't Jesus the world's greatest peacemaker? Absolutely. Does that mean He avoided conflict? Absolutely not! He continually confronted evil and hypocrisy. He cleansed the temple—not once, but twice. He levied scathing rebukes on the religious elite. All of Jerusalem rallied against Him and shouted for His crucifixion. But in an ironic twist, His death accomplished the peace God had desired all along, because He addressed the sin problem once and for all. "For it was the Father's good pleasure for all the fullness to dwell in Him (Jesus), and through Him to reconcile all things to Himself, having made peace through the blood of His cross" (Colossians 1:19–20 NASB).

We are all apprehensive about the unknown. We write the stories of our lives as we live them out—with no editing—and quite frankly, we are afraid of entering the conflict, because we don't know how it's going to turn out. We don't like the uncomfortable feeling of not being in control of every situation or circumstance. We cannot foresee how it will all unfold.

All of us must learn to trust God with the circumstances of our lives. Each of us needs to do all that we can do to make our situations better than they were before we arrived and trust God to use us to that end. But we must commit to the fact that we will arrive! We must show up on the scene and do whatever we can to help. We cannot drive in the opposite direction of the problem.

You know, God does something similar for us. He moves toward our conflicts when we call for help and backup. At our greatest points of need, we can count on the fact that God will be there for us. He said in Jeremiah 29:12 that "when you call on Me and come and pray to Me—I will listen to you." Is it not incredible to think that the God who created this universe has our backs? God is concerned about the circumstances of our lives, and He moves toward us. God moved toward our greatest conflict—sin —and did something for us that we could not do for ourselves. "For while we were still helpless, at the right time Christ died for the ungodly" (Romans 5:6 NASB). Now that's covering someone!

Jesus pronounced a blessing in the Beatitudes on those who would be peace officers. "Blessed are the peacemakers, for they will be called sons of God" (Matthew 5:9 NASB). To be called a child or son is the same as saying that person shares his or her father's nature. When Christians show love for their enemies, they exhibit the character of God Himself. What an honor it would be if, after observing our behavior of peace, someone would then say of us, "You look just like your Father." Since God is a God of peace (Romans 16:20, Hebrews 13:20), we will look like our Father when we become peace officers. Being called children of God is a worthy goal indeed!

Questions for discussion and a call to action:

1. Have you ever witnessed the escalation of a conflict? How did it go from bad to worse, and how was the conflict resolved?
2. What are some of the common characteristics of the peace-makers you know? Name the attributes and characteristics of Jesus that made Him the ultimate peacemaker.
3. Is there a difference between making peace and appeasement?
4. How might peace between two people be made easier when they themselves are at peace with God?
5. Is there some action you could take today to bring peace to a situation or circumstance that you have been avoiding?
6. Memorize Psalm 34:14: "Depart from evil and do good; seek peace and pursue it."

The Principle of Transfer
The Power of Making a Positive Difference

I n the police academy, one of the fundamental principles that we were taught concerning the investigation of a crime scene and the gathering of evidence was something called the "principle of transfer." The principle of transfer states that wherever there is contact between two objects, there is a transfer of material between those objects.

The principle of transfer involves the examination of items such as clothing, blood, carpet fibers, glass, hair, skin, dirt, and paint. The principle of transfer operates under the theory that something is brought to or taken away from every crime scene.

If a blue car hits a red car and then flees the scene of the accident, you can be assured that paint has been exchanged on both vehicles. Evidence was taken away from the scene (by the car that drove off), and evidence was left behind (on the car left at the scene). In the hit-and-run accident, there has been a transfer of evidence. It is a wise investigator who examines transfer evidence and links that evidence from victim to perpetrator. Today, there are numerous television programs that showcase forensic science and the principle of transfer.

I sincerely believe that the principle of transfer applies to each and every one of us in the realm of our influence. Every day, each of us comes into contact with our culture, and we will leave something and take something in every instance. God expects us to make a positive impact on humanity—to leave a godly impression on the people we contact.

Your life matters, and your influence is felt, even though you may not see it. Many people have given up on the idea that they have, can, and should make a positive difference in the lives of other people. When we leave a situation, it should be better than we found it. We should elevate conversations, not deflate them. We should attempt to bring out the best in the people around us and not the worst.

The ancient Greek philosopher Heraclitus is credited with saying, "No man ever steps in the same river twice, for it's not the same river and he's not the same man." Each time someone else stepped into the river, whether that person realized it or not at the time, the river was forever changed and would never be the same river again. What is true of rivers is also true of people. A different person emerges from each new interaction. A Christian's hope is that each interaction produces a better person rather than one who has been impacted negatively.

Ralph Waldo Emerson admitted, "Every man I meet is in some way my superior." He believed there was something he could learn in each encounter, and it led him to properly value every person he met. He also felt that "To laugh often and much; to win the respect of intelligent people and the affection of children … to leave the world a better place … to know even one life has breathed easier because you have lived. This is to have succeeded." Both Heraclitus and Emerson recognized the principle of transfer.

It would be sad and disappointing to live on this planet for fifty, sixty, or seventy years and have no positive evidence of the transfer. God has presented each one of us with a myriad of opportunities to touch the lives of people around us in a positive way. To fail to take advantage of those opportunities could have broader implications than we might realize.

Could it be, for instance, that the greatest crime any of us would ever commit would be to perpetrate a robbery against God? God asked in Malachi 3:8, "Will a man rob God? Yet you rob me." God resented that tithes and offerings were being withheld from Him; yet there are certainly other ways we can defraud God when we fail to be good stewards of the blessings and resources He gives to us. Don't rob God of the great potential He has placed in you by wasting your days. Don't steal the joy He could have of seeing you give yourself away in service to others as you live upon this earth. Maybe you have allowed some poor habit to steal away from you the positive aspect of this principle of transfer.

Booker T. Washington once said, "There is no power on earth that can neutralize the influence of a high, simple and useful life." I have always prayed that somehow, in some small way, God would use me, in my little corner of the world, to make a difference.

When I was in my early twenties, working as a police officer, I believed in what I was doing. I worked hard for the $16,000 a year I earned. I was proud to represent the city of West Palm Beach, and I was thankful for the opportunity that they afforded me. But more importantly, I believed that I had made a difference. I felt like the city was a little safer because of my presence. While I could not catch all the bad guys, I did catch a few. I could not save all the lives lost, but I did help save a few. I served my community and my God, and in doing so, I made a difference. And now, years later, I'm still praying that God will use me to make a difference. Jesus said,

> You are the salt of the earth. But if the salt loses its saltiness, how can it be made salty again? It is no longer good for anything, except to be thrown out and trampled underfoot. You are the light of the world. A town built on a hill cannot be hidden. Neither do people light a lamp and put it under a bowl. Instead they put it on its stand, and it gives light to everyone in the house. In the same way, let your light shine before others, that they may see your good deeds and glorify your Father in heaven. (Matthew 5:13–16 NIV)

Let's discuss what we should bring to the scene—not to the scene of the crime, but rather to every contact that we have with humanity. First, we should bring encouragement. "Therefore encourage one another and build each other up, just as in fact you are doing" (1 Thessalonians 5:11 NIV).

The world already has an abundance of discouragers. Discouragers bring you down, but encouragers build you up. Remember that discouragers remove the courage from your life, and encouragers instill courage. "And we urge you, brothers and sisters, warn those who are idle and disruptive, encourage the disheartened, help the weak, be patient with everyone" (1 Thessalonians 5:14 NIV).

Bring optimism. Look for the good and the positive in your life and in the lives of others. By definition, an optimist is somebody who tends to feel hopeful and positive about future outcomes. Robert Brault said that an optimist is "someone who isn't sure whether life is a tragedy or a comedy but is tickled silly just to be in the play." "'For I know the plans I have for you,' declares the LORD, 'plans to prosper you and not to harm you, plans to give you hope and a future'" (Jeremiah 29:11 NIV).

Bring integrity. A person of integrity is real and genuine. He or she is a whole person and not divided. People of integrity keep their promises and tell the truth. Even the enemies of Jesus had to admit that He was a man of great integrity: "Then the Pharisees went out and laid plans to trap him in his words. They sent their disciples to him along with the Herodians. 'Teacher,' they said, 'we know that you are a man of integrity and that you teach the way of God in accordance with the truth. You aren't swayed by others, because you pay no attention to who they are'" (Matthew 22:15–16 NIV). This was more than just flattery. These words were an honest evaluation of the life of Jesus by his enemies!

Bring a thankful spirit. It is difficult to be grateful and cynical at the same time. It's just about impossible to be thankful and critical in the same breath. Be appreciative of others. Paul said in Colossians 2:7 that we should be "overflowing with thankfulness."

"Let the peace of Christ rule in your hearts, since as members of one body you were called to peace. And be thankful. Let the message of Christ dwell among you richly as you teach and admonish one another with all wisdom through psalms, hymns, and songs from the Spirit, singing to God with gratitude in your hearts" (Colossians 3:15–16 NIV).

Bring kindness. "Therefore, as God's chosen people, holy and dearly loved, clothe yourselves with compassion, kindness, humility, gentleness and patience" (Colossians 3:12 NIV). "But love your enemies, do good to them, and lend to them without expecting to get anything back. Then your reward will be great, and you will be children of the Most High, because He is kind to the ungrateful and wicked" (Luke 6:35 NIV). Kindness is practicing the golden rule: "In everything, treat others as you would want them to treat you, for this fulfills the Law and the Prophets" (Matthew 7:12 NET).

Bring your involvement. You will get out of life what you put into life. You cannot and will not make a difference while standing idly on the sidelines of life. Make a contribution. It takes intentional effort to be salt and light. Scott Adams said, "You don't have to be a person of influence to be influential. In fact, the most influential people in my life are probably not even aware of the things they've taught me."

The same might have been said about the beloved character George Bailey from the classic movie *It's a Wonderful Life*. George came to a point where he felt his life was wasted. He was overcome with a feeling of insignificance and contemplated ending it all. Yet George was given the chance by a guardian angel named Clarence to see what life would have been like had he never lived. He relived a childhood experience in which he and his brother were playing in the snow, except in his vision, George was not there. His brother, Harry, sledded down the hill and was going so fast that he slid into the frozen lake. George discovered that had he not been there, Harry would have drowned, because George was the one who saved him.

It was George who kept his boss, Mr. Gower, a druggist grief-stricken over the untimely death of his son, from inadvertently giving poison pills to a sick family. It was George whose sacrifices to keep his father's loan business afloat prevented Mr. Potter,

Bedford Falls' cruel and corrupt banker, from taking control of the entire town and emptying it of hope and civility. He observed multiple events that convinced him that his life truly was one of significance. He had the opportunity to see his own contributions and what a truly great impact he had made.

The most powerful impact in history comes from individuals. Consider where we would be without the transfer of people like Thomas Edison, Alexander Graham Bell, George Washington, Henry Ford, Albert Einstein, Isaac Newton, Abraham Lincoln, and many others. Consider the spiritual legacy handed down to us from people of faith like Abraham, Noah, Ruth, Joseph, Moses, Paul, David, Esther, Daniel, Job, and Peter.

Even those whose names didn't make it into the biblical record continue to influence us today despite the fact that their contributions may have been considered unimportant at the time. Think of the little boy who shared his lunch with Jesus, the woman who put two small copper coins into the treasury, and the slave girl who informed Naaman of the powerful prophet in Israel.

I say all that leading up to the truth that the greatest event in all of history was the coming of an individual. You know that person to be Jesus. He only lived (physically) on this earth about thirty-three years. His ministry only lasted about three years. Yet the difference that He made is so incredible that the impact will be felt through all eternity. Jesus lived out the principle of transfer, and He calls us to do the same.

You can do this! You, too, can make a difference! You can bring encouragement, optimism, integrity, gratitude, kindness, and involvement into every encounter you have with others. You can resolve to treat each one you meet in a way that he or she leaves a better person than before his or her interaction with you. And you can be instrumental in pointing someone to Christ who might not have had that opportunity had you not been around. Leave each scene you enter with the positive evidence of your transfer.

Questions for discussion and a call to action:

1. Who has been a positive influence on your life? How did he or she influence you?

2. What did Jesus mean when He said, "Let your light shine before others, that they may see your good deeds and glorify your Father in heaven"? What goal does He want us to keep in mind with each interaction we have?

3. Can you give examples of how men and women of the Bible lived out the principle of transfer?

4. If, like George Bailey, you were given the chance to see what life would be like without your presence, how would the lives of those you are closest to be different? If your answer isn't what you want it to be, what can you do to change that?

5. Every day, ask God to use you to leave a godly influence on the lives of others. Instead of living your life so that you might be remembered, live your life so that it matters.

6. Memorize the golden rule: "In everything, treat others as you would want them to treat you, for this fulfills the Law and the Prophets" (Matthew 7:12 NET).

No One Has to Be a Career Criminal
The Power of Lasting Change

Have you ever heard the term "career criminal"? Not long ago in Miami, Florida, a man shot and killed two veteran detectives before he was gunned down. The newspaper called him a career criminal. The Encarta Dictionary defines *career* as "a job or occupation regarded as a long-term or lifelong activity." A career criminal is someone who has spent his or her entire life as a repeat offender. His or her sole occupation and full-time job is criminal activity. Many have made a career out of stealing or dealing drugs. But no one *has* to be a career criminal. A person may choose to be one, but he or she doesn't *have* to be one.

The prophet Jeremiah talked about how difficult it is for people to change in Jeremiah 13:23 (KJV) when he asked, "Can the Ethiopian change his skin, or the leopard his spots? Then may ye also do good, that are accustomed to do evil." Jeremiah was not talking about the impossibility of change but the extreme difficulty in making changes when you have grown accustomed and even been trained to do evil.

God's great news to humankind is that *people can change!* Of course, I am speaking about changing for the better. Is that not the point of the gospel—that God can change lives? Men, women, boys, and girls who are headed down a path of destruction can opt out of that path and choose a new path.

Not long ago, a brand-new Navy assault ship, the USS New York, arrived in its namesake city with a twenty-one-gun salute near the site of the 2001 terrorist attack. The big ship paused. Then the shots were fired with a cracking sound in three bursts. The ship is 684 feet long and can carry as many as eight hundred Marines. Its flight deck can handle helicopters and the MV-22 Osprey tilt-rotor aircraft.

What was so special about this ship? I read that the bow of that $1 billion ship, built in Louisiana, contains about 7.5 tons of steel from the fallen towers of the World Trade Center. During an interview, a woman who had lost a family member on September 11, 2001 commented about the USS New York, saying, "I'm proud that our military is using that steel." Then she paused and said, "It's a transformation ... from something really twisted and ugly."

The Encarta Dictionary defines *transformation* as "a complete change, usually into something with an improved appearance or usefulness; the act or process of transforming somebody or something."

God is in the transformation business. He has, can, and will take people and circumstances that are twisted and ugly and transform them into something solid and useful. Do you realize that present at the crucifixion of Jesus were not only His mother and other followers standing at a distance, but also—nearest to the cross of our Lord—was the classic contrast of cops and robbers?

The Bible teaches us that that Jesus was crucified between "two robbers" (Matthew 27:38, NASV). Also in front of Jesus stood a centurion, the Roman equivalent of the modern-day police officer. The Bible teaches that one of the two thieves remained callous of heart till his last breath, but the other changed his mind and heart. Jesus promised to be with him in Paradise that very day. Thieves can change, and they don't have to wait until the final hour of their lives to do so.

The officer who supervised the torture and crucifixion of Jesus that day changed as well. A few of the soldiers cast lots for Jesus' clothing and ignored the conversation of those dying men like they no doubt had done many times before. But this Roman centurion who watched Jesus die that day began to marvel at what had taken place. A centurion would have been in charge of at least eighty soldiers. He was the police captain, if you will. His conclusion to what he witnessed the day Jesus died, according to Luke 23:47, was, "Certainly this man was innocent." Mark wrote that when he "saw the way He breathed His last," he then stated, "Truly this man was the Son of God" (Mark 15:39 NIV). Matthew wrote that not only the centurion, but also "those who were with him keeping guard over Jesus, when they saw the earthquake and the things that were happening, became very frightened and said, 'Truly this was the Son of God!'"(Matthew 27:54 NASB)

People changed that day at the cross. A thief changed, and a centurion changed. And because of what happened at the cross, you and I can change, too. That is the good news God Himself promises. The outcome of the cross and the subsequent empty grave provided an avenue to real, lasting, eternal change!

Writing to the church at Ephesus, Paul said that they no longer had to steal, but instead, they could work. They no longer had to lie, but instead, they could tell the truth. They no longer had to speak words that tore down but could instead speak words that would build up. They no longer needed to be angry, but instead, they should be kind, tender, and forgiving (Ephesians 4:25–32). People can change. I have witnessed the transformation in my own life and in the lives of countless others.

The apostle Paul was a persecutor of the church, but by the power of God, he changed and became a preacher of the gospel (1 Timothy 1:12–16). Peter at one time denied that he even knew Jesus (Matthew 26:69–74), yet Peter changed and became one of the greatest billboards for what it means to speak up for Jesus when others try to silence you (Acts 4:18–19, 5:40–42).

Most of the folks who I arrested during my tenure as a police officer didn't stay in jail but were released. Some of those folks were determined not to repeat the same mistakes. They knew that their lives would not be judged by the moments of their offense and the arrest but by the total contributions of their lives. They changed! They became productive citizens who gave back to the state instead of unproductive inmates living off of the state. They learned some lessons from their poor choices and then made better choices. As a result, they will be remembered for what they would become and not for what they were when they did wrong.

I will never forget this lesson of change, as I witnessed it firsthand while preaching for a congregation in South Florida. A family of four attended every Sunday morning—a nice-looking couple with two boys. The man was obviously miserable. Have you ever seen a husband who was dragged to church? He was there because his wife wanted him there.

That man did everything he could to distract his young boys from the worship service. Our church placed small stickers on lapels to identify the visitors. He took those stickers off and stuck them on his eyelids during the Lord's Supper. His sons laughed, and his wife was embarrassed; yet they showed up Sunday after Sunday.

One Sunday, I preached a sermon from 1 Timothy 1:15 about Paul being the "chief of sinners"—how he was shown mercy and forgiveness and became an example for those who are serious about changing and receiving eternal life. When I offered the invitation, to my surprise, the man who had been such a distraction during my sermons stepped into the aisle, walked to the front of the building, and sat down on the front row. His head was hung low, and I could tell that he was crying. I knelt down beside him, put my hand on his shoulder, and asked him why he had come forward. He looked up at me with a seriousness that I had not witnessed in months and said, "I want to change. Harold, are you promising me that I can be forgiven like Paul was forgiven? Paul wasn't the chief of sinners; I am. Please tell me that God can change me, too."

When I baptized him that morning, he was still crying. I was crying. A soul was rescued from destruction, and another table setting appeared in heaven. A life was forever changed.

This man was a sign maker, and he also produced large canvases that covered some beautiful million-dollar yachts in Ft. Lauderdale. The Sunday following his baptism, he was back at worship, but this time with a smile that was contagious. That morning, he brought with him a large blue sign that had the word *AMEN* written across it. In my sermon that morning, every time I said something about Jesus or heaven, he held that sign up. Talk about distracting! I lost my place in my notes several times and started speaking to the opposite side of the auditorium.

When that sermon was over, he rolled up the sign and gave it to me. As he left, he said something about bringing his friends the next week and how great it was to be a Christian! When I think of change, I think of him. When I left South Florida to serve a church in Atlanta, he was the guy at the door who put the lapel stickers on visitors. He was the first to arrive for Bible school, and he was the last to leave following our worship services. By God's great power and grace, he was forever changed.

All of us need to change. None of us are so perfect that we couldn't make some important changes that would help us reach our God-given potential. Everybody needs to change something. There is not one soul on this planet who doesn't need to be forgiven and changed through the power of God. Romans 3:23 reminds us that "all sin and fall short."

Real and lasting change can only be accomplished with the strength and the power of God. God wants to transform us. "Therefore, I urge you, brothers and sisters, in view of God's mercy, to offer your bodies as a living sacrifice, holy and pleasing to God—this is your true and proper worship. Do not conform to the pattern of this world, but be transformed by the renewing of your mind. Then you will be able to test and approve what God's will is—his good, pleasing and perfect will" (Romans 12:1–2 NIV).

The word *transformed* in the original text is the Greek *metamorphoo,* from which we get the term "metamorphosis." It conjures up images of a caterpillar that enters a cocoon, later to emerge as a multi-colored butterfly. What God did for that caterpillar, He has in mind for you, only the morphing is into something much more beautiful. He wants to change you to look like His Son. "For those whom he foreknew he also predestined to be conformed to the image of his Son" (Romans 8:29 NASB). "My little children, for whom I labor in birth again until Christ is formed in you!" (Galatians 4:19 NKJV). Such a metamorphosis is not within our power. Positive thinking can carry us only so far. However, God has all the resources that you need to make and sustain lasting change.

Change can't occur without your permission; no one can make you change. The power comes from God, but He won't impose His will on you. Only you can stop making excuses and start taking responsibility for the outcome of your life. Only you can make the choice to initiate change in your own life. You must become an active participant in making the necessary changes in your behavior and attitudes. Stop waiting for someone to come along and do what only you can do with God's help and the guidance of His Word. You must want to change. Repentance is a change of heart that leads to a change of life.

Real and lasting change begins on the inside. Some of the most scathing words Jesus spoke during His short tenure on this earth were directed toward the religious leaders of His day when He said, "Woe to you, teachers of the law and Pharisees, you hypocrites! You clean the outside of the cup and dish, but inside they are full of greed and self-indulgence. Blind Pharisee! First clean the inside of the cup and dish, and then the outside also will be clean" (Matthew 23:25–26 NIV).

Jesus challenged the Pharisees by claiming that to appear righteous outwardly while being dirty inwardly was nothing more than hypocrisy. (I witnessed this many times in court. An intelligent attorney will tell his or her client to clean himself up before appearing before a judge. The client puts on a suit and combs his hair so that he appears respectable.) The only way you can thoroughly clean a cup on the inside is to wash it. So Jesus said that if want to change and be clean, then we must be washed on the inside. That's exactly what Ananias told Paul: "And now what are you waiting for? Get up, be baptized and wash your sins away, calling on His name" (Acts 22:16 NIV).

Paul considered himself the "chief of sinners," because he "was formerly a blasphemer and a persecutor and a violent aggressor" (1 Timothy 1:13). After realizing the error of his ways on the road to Damascus, he determined not to remain a repeat offender. Later on, that same Paul (who was baptized) wrote to Titus and said, "He saved us, not because of righteous things we had done, but because of His mercy. He saved us through the washing of rebirth and renewal by the Holy Spirit" (Titus 3:5 NIV).

You can change, and it's not too late! With God's help, you can start making those changes. You have much potential. God has given you gifts and opportunities. Change from the inside out, and allow God to wash you clean by the blood of His Son. Arise and be baptized, and wash away your sins!

Questions for discussion and a call to action:

1. Can you describe a person who you have personally known who by God's grace, made some drastic changes in his or her life? What positive changes has God helped you make in your own life?

2. Consider the dramatic nature of Paul's change—from blasphemer, persecutor, and violent aggressor to one who suffered for and contributed to the cause of Christ perhaps more than anyone else in history save Christ Himself. What might this man who referred to himself as the "chief of sinners" have to say to someone who believes he or she is beyond the point of change?

3. Cite some other biblical examples of radical transformation.

4. Name some contemporary examples of the Pharisees' hypocrisy of looking outwardly clean while being inwardly dirty (Matthew 23:25–26).

5. What sinful habit or errant attitude needs to be dealt with in your life right now? Surrender it to God. Ask God to help you take the mess you have helped create and make it His message.

6. Memorize Romans 12:2 (NIV): "*Do not conform to the pattern of this world, but be transformed by the renewing of your mind. Then you will be able to test and approve what God's will is—his good, pleasing and perfect will.*"

10

Every Mystery Solved; Every Case Closed
The Power of Personal Accountability

There is nothing more frustrating to a criminal investigator than a pending, unsolved crime. In an ideal world, all mysteries would be solved, and in every case, justice would be served. The problem, of course, is that we don't live in an ideal world. Every year in America and around the world, millions of crimes are committed that are never solved. According the Expanded Homicide Data (www.fbi.gov), an estimated 13,636 people were murdered nationwide in 2009. That would mean that on the average, in 2009, at least thirty-seven people were murdered every day in America. Many of these homicides remain unsolved. Some homicide cases draw national attention, but most are known only by the law enforcement personnel who are working them—and of course, the victims' families, who are still grieving.

You might recall the atrocious murder of young Adam Walsh. On July 27, 1981, six-year-old Adam Walsh was out with his mother when he disappeared from a Hollywood, Florida shopping mall. The extensive manhunt for the little boy lasted for two weeks. Suddenly, one afternoon, the case turned from a missing person to a homicide when two fishermen discovered Adam's severed head in a canal 120 miles due north from where Adam was abducted. The rest of his body was never found. On December 16, 2008, more than two decades later, Hollywood police announced that they had officially closed the Adam Walsh case and named Adam's killer as Ottis Toole, a prime suspect in the case who had twice confessed and recanted. Toole, a convicted pedophile and killer who associated with notorious serial killer Henry Lee Lucas, died in prison in 1996.

The Bible teaches that one day, every mystery will be solved, and every case will be closed. There is no such thing as an unsolved mystery as far as God is concerned. He knows every circumstance and every detail of every crime scene. He even knows motives. "The Lord searches every heart and understands every motive behind the thoughts" (1 Chronicles 28:9 NIV). God knows where to find hidden murder weapons and buried bodies. When God confronted Cain about the murder of his brother, Abel, "The LORD said, 'What have you done? Listen! Your brother's blood cries out to me from the ground'" (Genesis 4:10 NIV).

One day, all of the evidence will be presented, and justice will be served. "For God is greater than our hearts, and he knows everything" (1 John 3:20 NIV). People may think they have "gotten away with murder" on this side of eternity, but the final and highest court has not yet tried the case. And the charges that will be brought against us will not be heard by a jury of our peers but by God Himself. "You have set our iniquities before you, our secret sins in the light of your presence" (Psalm 90:8 NIV).

Jesus tells us that everything will be disclosed before God in the Day of Judgment.

> Meanwhile, when a crowd of many thousands had gathered, so that they were trampling on one another, Jesus began to speak first to his disciples, saying: "Be on your guard against the yeast of the Pharisees, which is hypocrisy. There is nothing concealed that will not be disclosed, or hidden that will not be made known. What you have said in the dark will be heard in the daylight, and what you have whispered in the ear in the inner rooms will be proclaimed from the roofs." (Luke 12:1–3 NIV)

One day, nothing will be concealed or hidden. What we have said in the dark and whispered in the inner room will be seen in the light of day and shouted from the rooftops. We can learn from this—first, that God is omniscient (all-knowing), but we still make the choice. "You know when I sit and when I rise; you perceive my thoughts from afar. You discern my going out and my lying down; you are familiar with all my ways. Before a word is on my tongue you, LORD, know it completely" (Psalm 139:2–4 NIV).

God knows your thoughts before you think them. He knows when you get up in the morning and when you go to bed at night. He knows your words before you speak them. And even though God knows what we are going to do, He does not manipulate us or take our free will from us.

Ray Prichard wrote in *His Eye Is on the Sparrow,*

> God sees and knows everything you do. He hears everything you say. Nothing escapes him. Everything is transparent before his eyes. Yes, you have free will, but you are 100% responsible

for every choice you make—that includes the choices you make in the words you say and the thoughts you think. He won't just judge the "big" things; he's going to judge the "little" ones, too.

Second, all of us are accountable to God. The writer of Hebrews said that "Nothing in all creation is hidden from God's sight. Everything is uncovered and laid bare before the eyes of Him to whom we must give account" (Hebrews 4:13 NIV).

> We sometimes like to think that we have moments of privacy when no one sees what we do or knows what we think. That may be true in reference to people, but this is not true of God. He sees in the inner room, even when the lights are out and when no one else can see. Respect for His knowledge and our accountability to Him means we will conduct our lives like an open book, where we have nothing to hide. (Darrell L. Bock, *The NIV Application Commentary: Luke,* (ZondervanPublishingHouse, 1996), 339)

One day, we will give an account to God for the stewardship of our lives. We will not have to answer for anyone but ourselves; yet each of us will answer for how we have spent and invested our time, money, and talents (Matthew 25:13–46).

Third, no one will escape judgment. "Just as people are destined to die once, and after that to face judgment, so Christ was sacrificed once to take away the sins of many; and he will appear a second time, not to bear sin, but to bring salvation to those who are waiting for him" (Hebrews 9:27–28). "Do not keep talking so proudly or let your mouth speak such arrogance, for the Lord is a God who knows, and by Him deeds are weighed" (1 Samuel 2:3 NIV).

Paul reminded the church at Corinth, "For we must all appear before the judgment seat of Christ, so that each of us may receive what is due us for the things done while in the body, whether good or bad" (2 Corinthians 5:10 NIV).

Jesus said in Matthew 16:27 (NIV), "For the Son of Man is going to come in his Father's glory with his angels, and then He will reward each person according to what they have done." We will either stand before Him as sinners who have been saved by the grace of God or we will stand before Him unsaved and unprepared to enter eternity.

Finally, we learn that life is not fair, but God is. We live in a world where innocent little boys are ruthlessly molested and murdered; crooked Enron executives drain millions of dollars out of a collapsing company, leaving longstanding employees with nothing in their retirement plans; bad things happen to good people; and good things happen to bad people. If we see these inequities occur all around us, how can we be sure that the Creator of life is fair?

Abraham instinctively knew God was a God of justice. After hearing about the coming wrath on the cities of Sodom and Gomorrah (one of which contained his own nephew, Lot, and his family), Abraham reasoned, "Far be it from You to do such a thing—to kill the righteous with the wicked, treating the righteous and the wicked alike. Far be it from You! Will not the Judge of all the earth do right?" (Genesis 18:25 NIV)

The psalmist declared, "Clouds and thick darkness surround Him; righteousness and justice are the foundation of His throne" (Psalm 97:2 NIV). While it appears to us in the here and now that certain deeds go unpunished, in the end, everyone will receive appropriate retribution for what he or she does. Paul claimed that God "has fixed a day in which He will judge the world in righteousness through a Man whom He has appointed" (Acts 17:31), and he entrusted his fate to that "righteous Judge" (2 Timothy 4:8).

The good news for Christians is that they will have someone to represent them on that final, fateful day in court. Not only will their Savior be their judge, but He will also be their defense attorney. They will have Jesus as an advocate; that is, Jesus will stand in their favor and support and testify on their behalf (1 John 2:1–2).

Something good that came out of the Walsh family tragedy. Of course, nothing is good about Adam's kidnapping and murder, but good is found in how the Walsh family responded in the days that followed Adam's death.

John Walsh, Adam's father, turned his grief into action, becoming an early advocate for missing children and crime victims. Three presidents—Ronald Reagan, George H. W. Bush, and Bill Clinton—honored John Walsh for his endeavors to safeguard children. The continued efforts of the Walsh family led to the passage of the federal Missing Children's Assistance Act of 1984, which established the National Center for Missing and Exploited Children.

In her article, "Tragedy Turned into Triumph," Jeanie Hamblen notes the following examples of people helping others after suffering great loss. "John Walsh turned his tragedy into *America's Most Wanted* after the horrific kidnapping and murder of his six-year-old son. As of January 5, 2011, the program has assisted in the capture of 1,136 criminals. John Walsh frequently ends the program with his trademark slogan, 'and remember, you can make a difference.'"

Mothers Against Drunk Driving began after thirteen-year-old Cari Lightner was killed in a hit-and-run by a drunk driver. Candy Lightner redirected her sorrow to create awareness and protect others. Amber Hagerman's abduction and murder inspired the formation of the nationally-known Amber Alert. According to *ABC News'* Emily Friedman, the program is credited with safely locating nearly five hundred children. I am not thankful for these terrible crimes and tragedies, but I am grateful for how the families of these victims responded to their personal tragedies.

One day, you and I will stand before our Maker, personally accountable for our lives. Preparation for that day starts now—today (2 Corinthians 6:2).

Questions for discussion and a call to action:

1. Does God's omniscience frighten or comfort you?
2. How should our attitudes and behaviors reflect the knowledge that we are ultimately accountable to God?
3. Read Psalm 73. Have you ever experienced some of the sentiments Asaph expressed—that sometimes life just doesn't seem fair? See if you can identify some truths Asaph acknowledged that helped him to resolve in his own mind that God knew what He was doing even though evil seemed to triumph in the here and now. What allowed him to say in the end, "Nevertheless I am continually with You; You have taken hold of my right hand" and "I have made the Lord God my refuge"?
4. Have you ever witnessed an individual or family turn their personal tragedy into a triumph?
5. What attitude or behavior do you possess right now that, if brought to light, would humiliate you? God already knows about it. Confess it, repent of it, and stop it!
6. Memorize Hebrews 4:14–16 (NASB): "Therefore, since we have a great high priest who has passed through the heavens, Jesus the Son of God, let us hold fast our confession. For we do not have a high priest who cannot sympathize with our weaknesses, but One who has been tempted in all things as we are, yet without sin. Therefore let us draw near with confidence to the throne of grace, so that we may receive mercy and find grace to help in time of need."

11

The Need for Authority
The Power of Personal Surrender

Vince Lombardi said that "football is like life—it requires perseverance, self-denial, hard work, sacrifice, dedication, and respect for authority." I'm thankful that I was raised in a home where the concept of authority was taught. I did not always feel that way, but with the wisdom of age and the experience I was afforded as a police officer, I have come to appreciate my parents more and more with every passing day.

We all answer to someone. We are all under someone's authority. As children, we were under the authority of our parents, then our teachers, and then later, our employers. We are under the authority of the police, the government, the IRS, the elders of our church families, and ultimately, we are all under the authority of God.

If you were not taught the value of authority in your home (which is where it should begin), then chances are that you will be taught the lesson of authority the hard way outside your home. I feel pity for the person who will spit on a teacher or run from the police. Maybe he or she was raised in a home where he or she did not learn respect for authority. It is a shame, because that person will inevitably learn the lesson of authority the hard way. Schools expel such a person, the police arrest him or her, and neither think that the person is funny or cute.

Have you been to juvenile court lately? You would be astonished by the seriousness of the crimes committed by young children. If you were able to sit and watch long enough, you would notice a disrespectful demeanor and the total disregard those children have for any kind of authority.

One Christmas, I worked an off-duty detail at a large department store in downtown West Palm Beach. I was called to the toy department in reference to three children causing a disturbance. I arrived in time to witness one of these children open the package of a new toy and then break the toy in half. Now I know how my dad must have felt, because I thought, *Someone is about to get thumped.*

I identified myself as a policeman, showed the kids my badge, and then asked them to find their parents or leave the store. Two of the three left immediately. But the one who stayed behind was not going to be told what to do by anyone, especially me. I escorted him to the front doors of the store, where just as he was about to leave, he made one more attempt to be insolent. He fell against the door and started yelling something about my trying to abduct him. After causing quite a scene and not rallying any sympathy or support from nearby customers, he cussed at me and left the store.

I didn't think much about the incident until a week or two later when a lawyer appeared at the police department to interview me for a possible lawsuit. This boy's parents wanted to sue me for having asked their son to leave the store. They said he received a small scratch on his arm when he fell against the door. It was only then that I realized that this kid didn't need to be thumped; his parents did!

Parents, please teach your children to respect authority. Realize that if they learn it at home, then when they go to school, they will in turn respect the teacher. If they are stopped by the police, then they will be respectful to the law. But ultimately, we want children to respect God's authority and learn to trust and obey His boundaries for their lives. All of this begins in the home.

"Discipline your children, for in that there is hope; do not be a willing party to their death" (Proverbs 19:18 NIV). "Children, obey your parents in the Lord, for this is right. Honor your father and mother—which is the first commandment with a promise— so that it may go well with you and that you may enjoy long life on the earth" (Ephesians 6:1–3 NIV).

People live with a false assumption—an illusion—that real happiness and freedom would come if there were no laws, rules, guidelines, or boundaries. This is a lie! Real freedom comes from living within the boundaries that God has given to us. Like a loving parent, God gives us those boundaries for our protection.

According to (www.dictionary.com) the word *authority* is defined as "1. The power to determine, adjudicate, or otherwise settle issues or disputes; jurisdiction; the right to control, command, or determine. 2. A power or right delegated or given; authorization: Who has the authority to grant permission? 3. A person or body of persons in whom authority is vested, as a governmental agency."

So what is authority? Simply put, authority is the right and ability to control, command, or determine the proper responses of others. Rebelling against lawful authority is nothing new. People have rebelled against authority since the beginning. According to Genesis 3, Adam and Eve had it all; yet they were challenged by Satan with the one tree from which they could not eat. They rebelled and were exiled from the garden.

An anti-authority attitude existed in Jesus' day. Jesus was amazed when he encountered a man who both respected authorities over him and exercised authority over others.

> The centurion heard of Jesus and sent some elders of the Jews to him, asking him to come and heal his servant. When they came to Jesus, they pleaded earnestly with him, "This man deserves to have you do this, because he loves our nation and has built our synagogue." So Jesus went with them. He was not far from the house when the centurion sent friends to say to him: "Lord, don't trouble yourself, for I do not deserve to have you come under my roof. That is why I did not even consider myself worthy to come to you. But say the word, and my servant will be healed. For I myself am a man under authority, with soldiers under me. I tell this one, 'Go,' and he goes; and that one, 'Come,' and he comes. I say to my servant, 'Do this,' and he does it." When Jesus heard this, he was amazed at him, and turning to the crowd following him, he said, "I tell you, I have not found such great faith even in Israel." (Luke 7:3–9 NIV)

I love the story about a government surveyor who brought his surveying equipment to a farm to do some work for the state and county by which he was employed. He knocked on the farmhouse door and asked the farmer for permission to go into one of his fields and take some readings. The farmer had no hospitality for any state or county officials, so he refused to give the man permission to work in any of his fields. He thought that maybe the government was going to take some of his land for a public project. "I will not give you permission to go onto my land!" said the farmer.

The surveyor then produced an official government document that authorized him to do the survey. "I have the authority," he said, "to enter any field in the entire country to do my work." Faced with the authority of the county, state, and federal government, the farmer unwillingly opened the gate and allowed the surveyor to enter one of his fields. The farmer then went to the far end of the field and opened another gate, through which one of his fiercest bulls came charging. Seeing the bull, the surveyor dropped his equipment and began to run for his life. The farmer shouted after him, "Show him that paper! Show him your authority!" (www. sermoncentral.com, "Submit to the Governing Authorities" by Michael Otterstatter)

There is a little bit of that farmer in all of us. That selfish child inside of us does not like being told what to do and where to stand. Our pride and flesh tend to resist authority. Whether it's giving the IRS its due or maintaining the speed limit on the highway, deep inside of each of us is a stubborn refusal to accept authority.

In his letter to the church at Rome, the apostle Paul presented a different attitude toward authority. Instead of rebelling and resisting, he said that in honoring authority, we honor God, and when we dishonor authority, we dishonor God.

Let everyone be subject to the governing authorities, for there is no authority except that which God has established. The authorities that exist have been established by God. Consequently, whoever rebels against the authority is rebelling against what God has instituted, and those who do so will bring judgment on themselves. For rulers hold no terror for those who do right, but for those who do wrong. Do you want to be free from fear of the one in authority? Then do what is right and you will be commended. For the one in authority is God's servant for your good. But if you do wrong, be afraid, for rulers do not bear the sword for no reason. They are God's servants, agents of wrath to bring punishment on the wrongdoer. (Romans 13:1–4, NIV)

What can you learn from the Romans 13 passage and this study on authority? First, God is the highest of all authorities. All authority belongs to God, because He is the Creator of all things. The hosts of heaven worship Him, saying, "You are worthy, O Lord, to receive glory and honor and power; for You created all things, and by your will they exist and were created" (Revelation 4:11 NKJV). Jesus said, "All authority in heaven and on earth has been given to me" (Matthew 28:18 NIV).

Do you remember what God said to King Nebuchadnezzar in his moment of pride? "You will be driven away from people and will live with the wild animals; you will eat grass like the ox and be drenched with the dew of heaven. Seven times will pass by for you until you acknowledge that the Most High is sovereign over all kingdoms on earth and gives them to anyone he wishes. The command to leave the stump of the tree with its roots means that your kingdom will be restored to you when you acknowledge that Heaven rules" (Daniel 4:25–26 NIV).

Second, God has established human authority. Whatever authority we may possess is a God-delegated authority. Paul said that governing authorities exist by God's establishment (Romans 13:3). God has established authority within the family and the home (Ephesians 5:22–32, Colossians 3:18–21). God has also established authority in the local church. Christ is the head of the church, ruling her by His Word (Ephesians 1:22–23, Colossians 1:18). Shepherds in the church oversee, rule, and lead (1Timothy 3:1–7).

Third, all human authority is limited. By definition, authority has a boundary or jurisdiction. It is possible to exceed and overstep the boundaries of authority. Police officers may have the authority or the right to arrest a criminal or write a speeding ticket but not to determine which television you buy.

On a Thanksgiving Day several years ago, my son was driving back to college for a late basketball practice when he was stopped by a highway patrolman and issued a citation for the tinting over the front windows of his truck. We had purchased the vehicle with the tinting already installed, and I assure you that shortly after he received that ticket, we were very prompt in removing the illegal tint. But something strange happened after the trooper handed my son the citation. As she turned to walk back to her car, she paused and began to question him about a bumper sticker on the back of his truck. What was strange about the whole conversation was that the bumper sticker was a pro-law enforcement emblem (a black square with a blue line running through it).

My son told her that his father had been a police officer and that his uncle worked for the Palm Beach County Sherriff's office, but the sticker was on the truck when he purchased it. The state trooper then informed my son that he needed to remove the sticker from the back bumper of his truck.

On that Thanksgiving Day, the state trooper had every right to stop my son and issue him a citation for the tinting. But she exceeded her authority by telling him to remove something that was not against the law (and quite frankly, none of her concern). Authority should be accompanied by integrity and responsibility.

Lack of character in leadership is just one of the reasons that people rebel against authority.

Finally, human authorities serve as God's agents. "For the one in authority is God's servant for your good. But if you do wrong, be afraid, for rulers do not bear the sword for no reason. They are God's servants, agents of wrath to bring punishment on the wrongdoer" (Romans 13:4 NIV). Paul reminded us that those in positions of authority and those who dispense justice are "ministers of God for good."

God has delegated authority to individuals in government and law enforcement, so when we submit to them, we submit, representatively, to Him. Robert E. Lee said, "Obedience to lawful authority is the foundation of manly character."

Paul reasoned that if people obey the law, they have nothing to worry about. But if they are disobedient, then they need to be afraid. If you are a law-abiding citizen, then you can drive from place to place in peace. But if you rob a bank or hurt a small child, then you need to be afraid, because the law will do its best to track you down and bring you to justice.

According to wise Solomon in the book of Ecclesiastes, crime should be punished and sentences carried out quickly as a deterrent: "Because the sentence against an evil deed is not executed quickly, therefore the hearts of the sons of men among them are given fully to do evil" (Ecclesiastes 8:11, NASV). This verse indicates that a failure to obey this principle has the effect of encouraging evil.

During Christmas, at the same department store where I had the run-in with the children destroying toys, I had another really strange experience. On one particular day, some of the store managers noticed a suspicious fellow going from department to department, charging less than fifty dollars' worth of merchandise and then taking the merchandise to his car, returning to the store, and repeating the process. (Back then, cashiers didn't run a check on a credit card if a purchase was under fifty dollars). When I questioned one department manager about the man, I found out that the man insinuated that he was a police officer and that when he had tried on a new suit jacket, this department manger noticed the man had handcuffs and also saw what he thought was a gun tucked into the waistband of his pants.

I cautiously followed the man around the store and into the parking lot. Then as he put his packages into the trunk of a rental car, I identified myself as a police officer and asked him if he was one also. When he said that he was not a police officer, I told him to put his hands on the car so that I could search him. As I pulled up his shirt, I saw the handcuffs and a gun. I immediately snatched the gun from his waist, and as I did, he hit me, shoved me away, and started to run. He was in his forties and in terrible shape. I was in my early twenties and in great shape. When he ran into rush-hour traffic on Dixie Highway, I was right behind him.

By this time, the store management had called the police station, and I could hear sirens in the distance. I knew help was on the way. I rapidly overtook the man, and when I caught up to him, I hit him just as hard as I could in the back of the head, and he went down like a sack of potatoes. He didn't resist after that, but my adrenaline was really pumping. This man was transported back to the station, where detectives would sort out all of his issues. The credit cards were stolen. The car he was driving was stolen, and when his real identity was revealed, we found that he had several outstanding warrants. That day, I was nothing more than one of "God's servants, agents of wrath to bring punishment on the wrongdoer."

It has been several years now since I served as a police officer, but you probably wouldn't be surprised to know that I still have great admiration and gratitude for those who wear the badge. They play a vital role in our society, executing their duties with delegated authority from God. We're made safer because these men and women are willing to put themselves in harm's way. They are deserving of our respect, thanks, and prayers.

> I urge, then, first of all, that petitions, prayers, intercession and thanksgiving be made for all people—for kings and all those in authority, that we may live peaceful and quiet lives in all godliness and holiness. This is good, and pleases God our Savior, who wants all people to be saved and to come to a knowledge of the truth. (1Timothy 2:1–4 NIV)

Questions for discussion and a call to action:

1. Have you ever witnessed disrespect of authority? What was the situation or circumstance, and what did you personally learn from the altercation?
2. What attitudes should accompany our submission to authority?
3. Does it strike you as odd that Paul made some of his statements in Romans 13 about the authority of government when the one he lived under would later call for his own beheading? Realizing that God is the ultimate authority (Acts 4:1–20), is there anything we can learn from Paul about submitting to authorities concerning matters we don't like but aren't necessarily contrary to the will of God?
4. What began the downward spiral of King Nebuchadnezzar's disrespectful attitude toward God's authority (Daniel 4:4–33)? What did the king acknowledge once his sanity was restored (Daniel 4:34–37)?
5. Do you possess a hidden, rebellious attitude toward your government, employer, or God? Ask God to help you humble yourself—right now—and willingly submit, trusting God as your ultimate authority.
6. Memorize James 4:6–8 (NASB): "But He gives a greater grace. Therefore it says, 'GOD IS OPPOSED TO THE PROUD, BUT GIVES GRACE TO THE HUMBLE.' Submit therefore to God. Resist the devil and he will flee from you. Draw near to God and He will draw near to you. Cleanse your hands, you sinners; and purify your hearts, you double-minded."

12

End of Watch—The Final Roll Call
The Power of Facing Death

In the world of law enforcement, when you hear the expression "end of watch," it usually refers to the untimely death of a fellow officer. Fire rescue and police departments use this expression at the conclusion of a funeral service or at the graveside of one of their fallen comrades. More often than not, "the end of watch" ceremony involves a radio transmission of the name, badge number, and date an officer began his or her service to the department and then concludes with the date of his or her death as the end of the officer's watch. Those who have witnessed this ceremony know how emotional the words "end of watch" can be for family, friends, and coworkers.

As a police officer, I witnessed many untimely deaths—lives cut short by accidents, acts of violence, or suicide. Death is final. There is no second chance and no reincarnation. As a minister, I have preached hundreds of funerals, including some for my own family. Because death is the final journey, it is imperative that we be constantly reminded that all will experience an end to our watch.

The Bible teaches that when viewed in its proper perspective, death can infuse us with wisdom for living. Listen to the wise words of Solomon in the book of Ecclesiastes: "A good name is better than fine perfume, and the day of death better than the day of birth. It is better to go to a house of mourning than to go to a house of feasting, for death is the destiny of every man; the living should take this to heart. Sorrow is better than laughter, because a sad face is good for the heart" (Ecclesiastes 7:1–3 NIV).

"Death is the destiny of every man; the living should take this to heart." With every funeral that you and I have attended, we were made privy to a powerful, motivating, life-changing message, and death was the teacher.

Wolfgang Amadeus Mozart said, "I thank my God for graciously granting me the opportunity of learning that death is the key which unlocks the door to our true happiness." You normally don't hear the words *death* and *happiness* used in the same sentence. But death is a key to unlocking many of life's greatest treasures with happiness being just one of them.

Everyone dies, and no one gets a free pass. Death is our destiny. That fact has already been determined, and it is unavoidable. Death can come at any time and at any age. We have no idea when death will call us. We do know, however, that death is on its way.

One of the funerals that I presided over a few years ago was that of a sixty-two year old woman named Judy. In late October, Judy was in her kitchen at 1:30 p.m. when a small airplane that had just taken off from a nearby airport crashed into her home. Her husband was upstairs and escaped with only a few scratches, but sadly, Judy and the pilot of that small plane were killed instantly. When I met with Judy's husband and their daughter prior to the funeral, they spoke of Judy with love and admiration. She was a loving wife and mother. As I listened to them tell me stories about Judy's life, I couldn't help but to think about how ordinary the day of Judy's death was. She and her husband woke up, showered, ate breakfast, laughed, and teased one another—and then it just happened. Somehow in the routine of their lives, death came. But that is what Solomon said, is it not? Death is the destiny of everyone.

We don't like to talk about death, but the Bible tells us that the acknowledgement of our own inevitable death is healthy and quite necessary in order for us to reach our fullest potential during our brief stay here on earth.

Steve Jobs, CEO of Apple Computer and of Pixar Animation Studios, delivered a commencement speech on June 12, 2005 at Stanford University. In that speech, Jobs spoke some extremely profound words to the graduating seniors about death!

When I was seventeen, I read a quote that went something like: "If you live each day as if it was your last, someday you'll most certainly be right." It made an impression on me, and since then, for the past thirty-three years, I have looked in the mirror every morning and asked myself: "If today were the last day of my life, would I want to do what I am about to do today?"

Remembering that I'll be dead soon is the most important tool I've ever encountered to help me make the big choices in life. Because almost everything—all external expectations, all pride, all fear of embarrassment or failure—these things just fall away in the face of death, leaving only what is truly important.

Remembering that you are going to die is the best way I know to avoid the trap of thinking you have something to lose. You are already naked. There is no reason not to follow your heart.

No one wants to die. Even people who want to go to heaven don't want to die to get there. And yet death is the destination we all share. No one has ever escaped it. And that is as it should be, because death is very likely the single best invention of life.

Steve Jobs believed what Solomon said many centuries ago. "Death is the destiny of every man and the living should take it to heart" (Ecclesiastes 7:2 NIV). Steve Jobs died on Wednesday, October 5, 2011 at the age of fifty-six. He brought us the iPod, iPad, and iPhone, but he admitted his own inventions were overshadowed by death.

What happens when the living take to heart the fact that death is the destiny of every man and woman? Why is it so important for us not to live in denial about our own forthcoming death or the death of our friends and loved ones? What can you learn from a funeral?

Death reminds us that our time on earth is limited. We are only here for a brief amount of time. The Bible tells us in the book of James that "you are a mist that appears for a little while and then vanishes" (James 4:14 NIV). As quickly as we arrive on earth, we vanish.

The Psalmist said, "Lord, make me to know my end, and what is the extent of my days; let me know how transient I am" (Psalm 39:4 NASB). All of us are transient! We are all passing through this life by brief stay or sojourn. Paul called our bodies an "earthly tent" in 2 Corinthians 5:1. That doesn't sound very permanent, does it?

Because life is short and our time is limited, then life must be lived with a sense of urgency. In John 9:4 (NIV), Jesus said, "As long as it is day, we must do the works of Him who sent me. Night is coming, when no one can work." Psalm 90:12 in the New Century Version says, "Teach us how short our lives really are so that we may be wise."

The following quotation is over two hundred years old and comes from the Quakers: "I expect to pass through the world but once. Any good therefore that I can do, or any kindness that I can show to any fellow creature, let me do it now. Let me not defer or neglect it, for I shall not pass this way again."

No matter how hard we might try, we cannot retrieve time; it never comes back to us. Time, as they say, marches on. When I drive away from a funeral service and head home or back to the church office, I feel a renewed sense of urgency about how I will spend my time, because my time is limited, and once lived, I can never get it back.

Benjamin Franklin said, "Dost thou love life? Then do not squander time, for that is the stuff life is made of." Don't procrastinate on living your life! Live with a sense of urgency!

Death reminds us to examine our priorities. Christian Gellert said that we all should "live as you will have wished to have lived when you are dying."

Funerals have a way of forcing us to define what is in reality the most important, valuable, and precious. If you knew that you only had one month to live, then you would not waste a precious second on trivial pursuits. The foresight of our death causes us to appraise our life.

Job said, "Naked I came from my mother's womb, and naked I will depart. The LORD gave and the LORD has taken away; may the name of the LORD be praised" (Job 1:21 NIV). Solomon said something similar in Ecclesiastes 5:15 (NIV): "Everyone comes naked from their mother's womb, and as everyone comes, so they depart. They take nothing from their toil that he can carry in their hands."

Life itself is a gift to be valued, cherished, and appreciated. Value your life. Stop taking for granted the blessing of breath, health, and opportunity. We all should view our lives as a gift from our Creator. Life is God's gift to us, and what we do with that life is our gift to Him.

I have seen much potential and talent buried in the cemetery and forever covered up. Some of those people died due to no fault of their own. But many of those deaths came because those folks never understood the precious gift that they were given, and they squandered it! They were given the gift of health and abused it. They were given the gift of a sound mind and fried it. They were given opportunity and wasted it. They were offered a blank canvas, and instead of attempting to paint a masterpiece, they littered it with graffiti.

Job said we arrive with nothing, and we can carry nothing with us when we leave. Death therefore reminds us of the depreciation of the material and the appreciation of the eternal. When faced with death, we think clearly about our priorities.

Death reminds us that we will leave an inheritance. Folk singer Joan Baez put it this way: "You don't get to choose how you're going to die, or when. You only get to choose how you're going to live now."

Go to a cemetery, and look at any gravestone. Underneath the name, you will see dates—for example, 1921–1984—a date of birth, a date of death, and a dash to represent everything in between. That's all this life really is—the short – between the time we arrive and the time we leave. What are you doing with the dash? How will you fill the – that will someday mark your gravestone? Plutarch observed, "The whole of life is but a moment of time. It is our duty, therefore to use it, not to misuse it."

In my church, we sing a song that says, "This world is not my home; I'm just a-passing through." It's important that all of us keep in the forefront of our thoughts the fact that this world is not our home and that we don't have much time. Because of that, we must redeem what time we do have as a precious gift.

On the last night I worked as a police officer, I spotted a black Ford with New York tags that was being sought nationally in connection with a homicide that was committed in New York. I stopped the Ford just inside our city limits, and the occupants gave up without incident. We had one of the two brothers being sought in custody and his car (which turned out to be part of the crime scene), which contained vital evidence of a murder.

Far too often, we hear about some disturbed individual who walks into a school or a fast food restaurant and kills people he or she has never met—the senseless taking of life with no regard to its value. The person's actions cut short someone else's life and removed from this earth that person's potential contribution.

King Hezekiah looked at death as a thief who would steal something of great value from him: "A writing of Hezekiah king of Judah after his illness and recovery: I said, 'In the prime of my life must I go through the gates of death and be robbed of the rest of my years?'" (Isaiah 38:9–10) Death in the prime of our life truly is a thief! Death robs us of any future contribution.

In the movie *Unforgiven*, Clint Eastwood plays a retired Old West gunslinger named William Munny who reluctantly takes on one last job with the help of his old partner and a young man. There is a scene toward the end of that movie in which William Munny is asked what it's like to kill a man. He replies, "You take away all that he is and all that he is ever going to be."

We should not only value life, but also value our lives. Take care of yourself physically. Take advantage of your opportunities. A few minutes ago, as I wrote the words "evidence of a murder," I thought about God investigating us to see if we left behind any evidence of a life. Are we leaving anything significant behind that links us to our temporary stay on this planet? Are we redeeming the time and using it wisely? Are we cherishing this gift called life?

When our children, Larry and Michelle, were young my wife, Kay, and I took them to Disney World. One of my favorite venues was called the Carousel of Progress. The Carousel of Progress was sponsored by General Electric at the time. We sat in a revolving stadium to witness the progression of technology through the years. My wife and children always asked me why I liked to watch that show so much. I liked it because it was nostalgic and sentimental (and air-conditioned)! It made me think about my childhood, grandparents, and great grandparents.

I also loved a song that played over and over as we watched the animatronics on stage: "The Best Time of Your Life," written by Richard M. Sherman and Robert B. Sherman in 1974. The words of the song lifted my spirits and made me want to cherish every minute of my life. "Now is the time, now is the best time, now is the best time of your life! Life is a prize, live every minute, open your eyes and watch how you win it!" The Disney World trip was over twenty years ago, and I can still hear the tune of that song in my head. But more importantly, I still appreciate the theme of the Sherman brother's song: life is a prize; live every minute. Those are wise words.

Death is the destiny of every man and woman. For all of us, there is a final roll call. We must redeem the time we are given. In the end, we must be ready.

Questions for discussion and a call to action:

1. In John 9:4, Jesus said, "Night is coming when no man can work." How did Jesus demonstrate this sense of urgency in His life and ministry?

2. How would you behave differently if you knew you had a very limited amount of time to live?

3. Paul's challenged each of us in Ephesians 5:15 to "make the most of your time, because the days are evil." Name the individuals in Scripture who you believe stepped up to that challenge.

4. What kind of inheritance do you think is more important and lasting to leave to your children or descendants—one that is monetary or one that is spiritual in nature? Of these two, which do you spend the most time and effort preparing?

5. Considering the brevity of life and the inevitability of death, what do you need to do today that you have been putting off? Make that apology. Write that letter, or make the phone call. Give that gift. Give your life to God, and allow Him to redeem it. Stop procrastinating. Night is coming, so do it now!

6. Memorize Psalm 118:24 (NASB): "This is the day which the Lord has made; Let us rejoice and be glad in it."

13

Putting Your Life on the Line
The Power of a Committed Life

On March 30, 1981, President Ronald Reagan delivered a speech to the Construction Trades Council at the Washington Hilton Hotel. Ronald Reagan had been elected as the nation's fortieth President for only sixty days. After the President's speech, the Secret Service detail assigned to protect the President walked in a formation around him. As the agents left the hotel and were only a few feet from placing the President into an armored limousine, John Hinckley, Jr. rushed out of a nearby crowd of bystanders, firing a .22 caliber gun. Hinckley fired six rounds in just a few seconds. Four of the six bullets struck someone.

As you might recall, one of the bullets struck the President; another seriously injured his Press Secretary, James Brady. Two law enforcement officers were also injured in the shooting. Police officer Thomas Delahanty was shot in the neck, and Secret Service Agent Timothy McCarthy was hit in the abdomen. Video of the event shows Secret Service Agent Timothy McCarthy turning into

Hinckley's line of fire and placing himself in front of the President, preventing any further bodily harm to President Reagan.

During a television interview, Tim McCarthy told *The Early Show* co-anchor Rene Syler,

> In the Secret Service, we're trained to cover and evacuate the President. And to cover the President, you have to get as large as you can, rather than hitting the deck. So I have to say ... it probably had little to do with bravery and an awful lot to do with the reaction based upon the training. It was a heck of a team effort out there that day. It was people like Ray Shaddock and Jerry Parr, pushing the President into the car, other agents going to John Hinckley and helping subdue him, to help save the life of the President.

McCarthy, who fully recovered from his wounds, received the Award of Valor in 1982 in recognition of his bravery. He is currently the police chief of Orland Park, Illinois.

When I hear stories like this, I begin to wonder if I am willing to sacrifice everything for my Lord and Savior. If McCarthy could have that kind of dedication and commitment to a President who he was assigned to protect, what sort of dedication should I possess as a servant of the Creator of the universe? Jesus said, *"No one after putting his hand to the plow and looking back,* is fit for the kingdom of God"* (Luke 9:62 NASB).

When Jesus exhorted His followers to "put their hand to the plow," He was not challenging them with a career in farming. Jesus was issuing the great challenge of discipleship: "Whoever wants to be my disciple must deny themselves and take up their cross daily and follow me" (Luke 9:23 NIV). Following Jesus in discipleship is putting your hand to the plow. Jesus spoke those "hand to the plow" words of Luke 9:62 in the context of a discussion with some want-to-be followers who did not understand the depth of commitment they would need to make.

To put your hand to the plow is to undertake a task, get down to business, and embark on a course of action. Putting your hand to the plow is a call to commitment. "Hand to the plow" implies a start. It means you have stopped talking about plowing and have started plowing. You are actually working.

In Luke 10, Jesus appointed seventy and sent them out in pairs ahead of Him. Luke 10:2 (NASB) states, "And He was saying to them, 'The harvest is plentiful, but the laborers are few; therefore beseech the Lord of the harvest to send out laborers into His harvest.'" (This is the same request that Jesus made of the twelve in Matthew 9:37–38.)

The Lord asked His followers to pray for workers—for laborers. Jesus wanted to send out workers, laborers—not spectators—into His harvest. This plowing, sowing, and reaping is hard work. It's arduous and demanding work on the farm, and it is difficult and challenging work in the kingdom.

"Hand to the plow" also implies servitude. The committed follower of Christ should understand that being a Christian is to be called into God's service. It means to serve God. The notion of service behind this agricultural picture is found in many places in the New Testament. For example, in Luke 17:7 (NKJV), the Christian is spoken of as a servant of God plowing the field. "And which of you, having a servant plowing or tending sheep, will say to him when he has come in from the field, 'Come at once and sit down to eat'?"

The work being done is not to benefit the servant but rather the one he or she serves. Yes, the servant will earn his or her daily wage in providing services, but the master is the one who owns the field, dictates the work, and controls the produce that is derived from the labor.

Realizing this, what Luke related as he continued makes perfect sense. "He (the master) does not thank the slave because he did the things which were commanded, does he? So you too, when you do all the things which are commanded you, say, 'We are unworthy slaves; we have done only that which we ought to have done'" (Luke 17:9–10 NASB). Because the Christian has put his or her hand to the plow, he or she understands that the duty and role is one of service to the Master.

Further, "hand to the plow" implies sacrifice. The decision to follow Jesus would be a very deliberate one in which known sacrifices would be made. In the words just prior to Luke 9:62, Jesus illustrated what those wishing to put their hands to the plow would relinquish as they became followers of Him. In verse 58, a disciple gave up any claims to home and security. "The foxes have holes and the birds of the air have nests, but the Son of Man has nowhere to lay His head."

Luke 9:59–61 points out that even family ties might have to be severed if they represented a priority taking precedence over following Christ. That is not surprising considering what Jesus would also say in Luke 14:26 (NASB); "If anyone comes to Me, and does not hate his own father and mother and wife and children and brothers and sisters, yes, and even his own life, he cannot be My disciple." Sacrifice could involve losing one's own life in the process—something the image of a cross would also undoubtedly convey (Luke 9:23).

"Hand to the plow" implies stepping forward. Continuing to look back disqualifies us. In the Greek text, this verb is a present participle that expresses a continuous action. "If any man puts his hand to the plow and keeps looking back, this person is not fit for the kingdom." It is not just an occasional backward glance. He is constantly looking back. According to Jesus, when we look back, we become someone who is not fit or of no use to the kingdom of God.

When a farmer puts his or her hand to the plow, he or she looks, thinks, and moves forward. You cannot look back when you are called to step forward. In fact, if your gaze is behind you as you plow, how likely are you to plow a straight row? Jesus knows what He is talking about—not just in the work of a farmer, but also in the work of a Christian.

Jesus does not ask us to do something that He was unwilling to do. Jesus made this kind of commitment and demonstrated this kind of determination. "Now it came to pass, when the time had come for Him to be received up, that He steadfastly set His face to go to Jerusalem" (Luke 9:51 NKJV). Jesus displayed His total commitment to us at Calvary.

After Moses leads the nation of Israel out of Egypt following four hundred years of oppression, one might think that they would be appreciative and grateful. But instead, all they could do was longingly look back at Egypt.

The whole congregation of the sons of Israel grumbled against Moses and Aaron in the wilderness. The sons of Israel said to them, "Would that we had died by the Lord's hand in the land of Egypt, when we sat by the pots of meat, when we ate bread to the full; for you have brought us out into this wilderness to kill this whole assembly with hunger. (Exodus 16:2–3 NASB)

The people of Israel had already witnessed the parting of the Red Sea and the destruction of Pharaoh's army, but all they could do was reflect on what they left behind in Egypt.

Have you noticed that the people who lack commitment tend to be complainers? Moses certainly noticed. Moses was far from perfect, but he displayed the character of a committed man. Remember, Moses had also turned his back on Egypt.

> By faith Moses, when he had grown up, refused to be known as the son of Pharaoh's daughter. He chose to be mistreated along with the people of God rather than to enjoy the fleeting pleasures of sin. He regarded disgrace for the sake of Christ as of greater value than the treasures of Egypt, because he was looking ahead to his reward. By faith he left Egypt, not fearing the king's anger; he persevered because he saw him who is invisible. (Hebrews 11:24–27 NIV)

Moses knew what it was like to put his hand to the plow. Instead of looking back to Egypt, he looked ahead to his reward.

When God made arrangements for Lot and his family to be rescued from Sodom prior to its destruction, He gave orders for all who would be rescued to not look back at the city (Genesis 19:17). But Lot's wife looked back at the city and became a pillar of salt (Genesis 19:26). In the New Testament, when Jesus mentioned Lot's wife, it was in the context of His second coming and discipleship. "It will be just the same on the day that the Son of Man is revealed. On that day, the one who is on the housetop and whose goods are in the house must not go down to take them out; and likewise the one who is in the field must not turn back. Remember Lot's wife. Whoever seeks to keep his life will lose it, and whoever loses his life will preserve it" (Luke 17:30–33 NASB).

There is something about looking back that demonstrates to God a lack of commitment. When a man comes to the marriage alter and he is about to speak vows of promise and commitment to his future wife, I promise you, she does not want him to look back.

A man's future wife will not want a groom who is thinking about the single life he is leaving behind—only the future they have together moving forward. And the same thing could be said of a man who is watching his bride coming down the aisle toward him. Can you imagine the feeling that would come over a future husband if his future wife was looking for someone else while walking toward him? God's call of commitment is one that looks ahead and could include removing anything that would hinder the forward motion of discipleship.

According to 1 Kings 19, when Elisha was called by Elijah, Elisha was plowing and made a request of Elijah.

> So he departed from there and found Elisha the son of Shaphat, while he was plowing with twelve pairs of oxen before him, and he with the twelfth. And Elijah passed over to him and threw his mantle on him. He left the oxen and ran after Elijah and said, "Please let me kiss my father and my mother, then I will follow you." And he said to him, "Go back again, for what have I done to you?" So he returned from following him, and took the pair of oxen and sacrificed them and boiled their flesh with the implements of the oxen, and gave it to the people and they ate. Then he arose and followed Elijah and ministered to him. (1 Kings 19:19–21 NASB).

Talk about commitment! Elijah apparently sensed that Elisha's request was not an excuse or one that suggested either delay or insincerity. It was, in reality, quite the opposite. Elisha sacrificed and gave away all that he had before joining Elijah in the service of the King. There was no returning to farming after such a great commitment. With no plow and no oxen to pull the plow, there was also no hindrance to the task ahead of him. Elisha had indeed "put his hand to the plow"—just one of a different kind.

Paul spoke about this power of commitment, leaving behind certain things, and moving toward his spiritual goal in Philippians 3:13–14 (NASB); "Brethren, I do not regard myself as having laid hold of it yet; but one thing I do: forgetting what lies behind and reaching forward to what lies ahead, I press on toward the goal for the prize of the upward call of God in Christ Jesus."

Daniel 3 tells of three Hebrew men who were thrown in a fiery furnace because they refused to bow down to a golden idol. These men were willing to die rather than compromise their faith. Their response to the king in the face of death was this: "If it be so, our God whom we serve is able to deliver us from the furnace of blazing fire; and He will deliver us out of your hand, O king. But even if He does not, let it be known to you, O king, that we are not going to serve your gods or worship the golden image that you have set up" (Daniel 3:17–18 NASB). They were committed, and there was no turning or looking back!

The early followers of Jesus were willing to lay down their lives in order to preach to others about the resurrection of Jesus.

After calling the apostles in, they flogged them and ordered them not to speak in the name of Jesus, and then released them. So they went on their way from the presence of the Council, rejoicing that they had been considered worthy to suffer shame for His name. And every day, in the temple and from house to house, they kept right on teaching and preaching Jesus as the Christ. (Acts 5:40–42 NASB)

Again, this is exactly what Jesus had in mind when He said, "If anyone wishes to come after Me, he must deny himself, and take up his cross daily and follow me. For whoever wishes to save his life will lose it, but whoever loses his life for My sake, he is the one who will save it" (Luke 9:23–24 NASB).

I'm not suggesting that our lives are a form of gambling, but in poker, the player who goes "all in" lays every bit of money—all of the chips he or she possesses—on the table. In the same way, I believe that Jesus insisted that we as His followers live "all in." Every day, you and I should take everything we have—everything we are—lay it down on the table of faith, and say to God, "I am all in! Lord, I'm not going to hold or keep anything back from you. I give it *all* to you. My possessions, talent, time, potential—all of it belongs to you. I am putting my hand to the plow, and I am putting my life on the line. I want to live every day to bring glory to you."

I love these challenging words written by W. H. Murray, a Scottish Mountaineer and author:

Until one is committed, there is hesitancy, the chance to draw back, always ineffectiveness. Concerning all acts of initiative and creation, there is one elementary truth the ignorance of which kills countless ideas and splendid plans: that the moment one definitely commits oneself, then providence moves too. All sorts of things occur to help one that would never otherwise have occurred. A whole stream of events issues from the decision, raising in one's favor all manner of unforeseen incidents, meetings and material assistance which no man could have dreamed would have come his way.

I have learned a deep respect for one of Goethe's couplets: "Whatever you can do, or dream you can, begin it! Boldness has genius, magic, and power in it." (W. H. Murray in *The Scottish Himalaya Expedition*, 1951)

Questions for discussion and a call to action:

1. The people of Israel looked back at Egypt, and Lot's wife looked back at Sodom. What are you dwelling on that needs to be left behind?

2. Elisha burned up his plow and slaughtered his oxen. What might need to be taken out of the way so you can fully put your hand to Christ's plow?

3. Of the four components discussed—starting, servitude, sacrifice, and stepping forward—which do you find the most difficult part of putting your hand to the plow?

4. The Bible teaches, "Commit your works to the Lord and your plans will be established" (Proverbs 16:3). How can we apply this truth to our daily lives?

5. What are the qualities of a truly committed disciple?

6. Memorize Galatians 2:20 (NASB): "I have been crucified with Christ; it is no longer I who live, but Christ lives in me; and the life which I now live in the flesh I live by faith in the Son of God, who loved me and gave Himself for me."

7. Finally, tell God that you are ready to live "all in." Move beyond words to actions. Tell Him, "I surrender! I don't want to fight your will for my life any longer. I repent of my sins and I am ready for a future with you as the Lord of my life. I am ready to put my hand to the plow." If you are willing to pray these words to our heavenly Father, then if you haven't already obeyed the gospel, do as Ananias encouraged Saul in Acts 22:16 (NASB): "Now why do you delay? Get up and be baptized and wash away your sins, calling on His name."

CPSIA information can be obtained at www.ICGtesting.com
Printed in the USA
LVOW040246080113

314730LV00002B/147/P